# RETREAT WITH THE LORD

# Retreat with the Lord

*A Popular Guide to the Spiritual Exercises of Ignatius of Loyola*

## John A. Hardon, S.J.

CHARIS

Servant Publications
Ann Arbor, Michigan

Scripture texts used in this work are usually taken from the *New American Bible with Revised New Testament,* copyright © 1986 Confraternity of Christian Doctrine. All rights reserved. Occasionally, Scripture texts are taken from *The Jerusalem Bible,* copyright © 1966 by Darton, Longman & Todd, Ltd. and Doubleday & Company, Inc. Such citations are noted by the parenthetical reference (JB).

Published by Servant Publications
P.O. Box 8617
Ann Arbor, Michigan 48107

Published with the permission of Superiors
V. Rev. Joseph Daoust, S.J.
Provincial, Detroit Province of the Society of Jesus, 1993

Cover design by Gerald Gawronski/ The Look
Cover illustration by James D. Adams

97   10   9   8   7   6

Printed in the United States of America
ISBN 0-89283-833-7

**Library of Congress Cataloging-in-Publication Data**

Hardon, John A.
   Retreat with the Lord : a popular guide to the Spiritual exercises of Ignatius of Loyola / John A. Hardon.
      225 p.   cm.
      ISBN 0-89283-833-7
      1. Ignatius, of Loyola, Saint, 1491-1556. Exercitia spiritualia.
2. Spiritual exercises.  3. Retreats.  I. Title.
BX2179.L8H33   1993
248.3–dc20                                                    93-25754

# Contents

# Acknowledgments

MY PRAYERFUL GRATITUDE TO THOSE who made this volume possible.

To David Came and his co-workers of Servant Publications for their generous cooperation in editing and preparing the manuscript for press.

To Michael Breslin and his wife Carole Breslin for their many dedicated hours of typing and proofreading.

To my Jesuit Provincial, Very Reverend Joseph Daoust, S.J., for his *Imprimi Potest*.

To the Marian and Ignatian Catechists for the inspiration they gave by making the thirty-day Spiritual Exercises of St. Ignatius, and encouraging others to do the same.

To those who kindly gave their endorsement to the publication of this manual.

Special thanks are due to those who provided the Ignatian and other saintly maxims, notably Pascal Parente, *The Well of Living Waters*; Ronda Chervin, *Quotable Saints*; Louis Kaczmarek, *Hidden Treasure*; and Gabrial Hevenesi, *Scintillae Ignatianae*.

# What Are the Spiritual Exercises?

IN HIS OWN WORDS, the Spiritual Exercises of St. Ignatius are a carefully planned "method of examination of conscience, of meditation, of vocal and mental prayer, and of other spiritual activities." This describes the Spiritual Exercises in terms of what they consist of or what the person making the Exercises is expected to do. Their purpose is also identified by their author. They are a "way of preparing and disposing the soul to rid itself of all inordinate attachments and, after their removal, of seeking and finding the will of God in the disposition of our life for the salvation of our soul."

Ignatius compares the Spiritual Exercises to bodily exercises like "taking a walk, journeying on foot, and running." The comparison is useful. We take bodily exercise in order to strengthen the bodily muscles, our bodily circulation, and the function of the heart. So the Spiritual Exercises are meant to strengthen our faculties of the soul, to enlighten the mind, and inspire the will to operate more effectively.

Moreover, and more importantly, the Spiritual Exercises have a definite goal. They are to help us remove our sinful addictions, as we may call them. Once these are removed, the Exercises are to dispose us to want to learn what God expects of us, discover his will, and then determine to put it into practice.

The expression "want to learn" is not casual. Our bad habits are not only ingrained through frequent yielding to our fallen

9

inordinate – unusual or excessive

human nature. They blind us to even recognizing that we have bad inclinations. The Exercises therefore have as their first purpose to open our eyes to our own sorry condition. With God's grace, they enable us to want to look at the humiliating side of ourselves. Unless we recognize our moral weakness, we will lack the humility necessary to cooperate with the grace of God. This is no small matter because our natural bent is to see what is praiseworthy in our character and to admire our own virtues.

However, that is only the beginning. In making the Exercises we should beware of getting preoccupied with our failings, no matter how deep or serious these may be. Why? Because we can become overwhelmed by our weaknesses and, as a result, not recognize our capacity for good. In other words, we should aim at obtaining a balanced perspective of our relationship with God.

An honest appraisal of our sinful tendencies is the precondition for discovering the will of God. This should not be surprising because what most obscures our seeing the will of God is preoccupation with our own will.

Note that Ignatius does not leave this "will of God" in the abstract. He says that we are to find the divine will "in the disposition of our life for the salvation of our soul." This means that we are to find out how God wants us to dispose, that is, arrange or organize our life in order to reach heaven.

## THE ROLE OF THE DIRECTOR

As St. Ignatius understood the Exercises, someone should direct whoever uses the Exercises to make them properly. Consequently, making the Exercises in private does not exclude a director. Persons who have made the Exercises for years under competent direction may dispense with the immediate direction that is the normal procedure. But this is an exception.

A private Ignatian retreat, therefore, may mean several things:

- A retreat made privately and not as part of a group.
- A retreat made alone, where the director provides what are called the "points" or outline for each meditation and also

regularly meets with the retreatant for guidance.

- A retreat made alone, where the director does not personally give the points. His role is to keep in contact with the retreatant daily or every so many days to guide the soul of the person making the Exercises.

This manual is mainly designed for those making the Exercises by themselves, but under someone who provides the necessary direction. Contact with the director may be by either telephone or correspondences or both.

To be stressed is that some ongoing direction is required. The reason is that the Exercises are a supernatural means of knowing and cooperating with the divine will. In the language of Catholic Christianity, the Church is the necessary channel of the grace needed to know and choose God's will. Concretely, therefore, someone representing or speaking for the Church is the instrument through whom God provides the graces of enlightenment for the mind and of inspiration for the will.

A copy of the Spiritual Exercises is indispensable for making the retreat. It will provide directives, scriptural references, and information which the present manual presumes are available to the retreatant. The best English translation of the Exercises, on which this manual is based, is published by Loyola University Press in Chicago.

St. Ignatius is quite detailed in his directives for the one who guides the Spiritual Exercises. How are these Ignatian directives to be understood in a private retreat? The following are some recommendations:

- Given the limitations of time and frequency of contact with the retreatant, the director should be as precise and definite as possible.
- The retreatant should be encouraged to keep a spiritual journal during the retreat. This will help to select the main issues of each meditation and enable the director to focus on the essential needs of the retreatant.
- The retreatant should carefully read the Introductory Ob-

servations given by St. Ignatius as his prelude to the Exercises. They are invaluable for both the one making and the one giving the retreat. They are especially useful for the person making a private retreat. They can at least partially supply for the more detailed guidance that is presumed unavailable in a private retreat.

## THE MEANING OF THE FOUR WEEKS

There is an obvious logic to the Spiritual Exercises. They have a definite goal and provide definite means for reaching it. This logic is already expressed in the sequence of meditations to be made, the order in which they are to follow, and the relationship among the meditations.

That is why, as St. Ignatius explains, "Four weeks are assigned to the Exercises." This does not mean that each week must be seven days long. Much depends on the disposition of the one making the Exercises. Some people are "slower in attaining what is sought." Or again, "some may be more diligent than others, and some are more disturbed and tried by different spirits."

Adjustment of the number of days for each week depends on all the foregoing factors. "However, the Exercises should be finished in approximately thirty days."

Each week has its own purpose, which, in turn, becomes the means for the purpose of the week following. The final week thus becomes the culmination of the preceding three weeks.

**The First Week.** The first week "is devoted to the consideration and contemplation of sin." This does not mean that the whole week is exclusively preoccupied with sin. It means that, except for sin, there would have been no need for redemption, nor would there be any certain reason for the incarnation. And, consequently, there would have been no revealed grounds for the coming of Christ or the institution of the Church or, in fact, for Christianity.

**The Second Week.** The second week concentrates on "the life of Christ, Our Lord, up to Palm Sunday inclusive." This week is not only the longest and most detailed part of the Exercises, but it also summarizes everything that Christian spirituality stands for. It spans everything in the life of Christ from his conception at Nazareth to his glorious entry into Jerusalem on Palm Sunday.

Surprisingly, the second week is introduced by the kingdom meditation which gives the key to understanding the following of Christ. We are to follow him in the imitation of his virtues. But why? In order to be sent by him into the world for the salvation of others.

Within the second week are the key meditations of the Spiritual Exercises: the Two Standards, the Three Classes of People, and the Three Kinds of Humility. All of these are preliminary to the Election or Choice, which is the heart of the Ignatian retreat.

**The Third Week.** The third week is very short in the text of the Exercises, but it spans the longest sustained narrative in the Gospels. The passion of Christ, from the Last Supper to Calvary covers less than twenty-four hours. Yet accumulatively the evangelists devote no less than five hundred ninety-two verses to the historic events which determined the destiny of the human race.

This week appropriately closes with a set of rules with regard to eating. The practice of mortification in food and drink has been associated over the centuries with the passion of Christ. The Lenten season and Friday abstinence go back to the early Church.

**The Fourth Week.** The fourth week is devoted to the resurrection of Christ and his appearances from Easter Sunday to Ascension Thursday. Opening this week is a contemplation on Our Lord's appearance to his mother, and closing with the climactic contemplation to attain love of God. As an appendix to the fourth week, St. Ignatius gives the Three Methods of Prayer. They provide a variety of ways to communicate with the risen and glorified Savior, besides directly meditating on the historical events of his earthly life.

## WHAT IS A RETREAT?

Historically, a retreat is a withdrawal for a period of time from one's usual surroundings and occupation to a place of solitude in order to make certain necessary decisions in the spiritual life. In this sense, retreats are as old as Christianity. In fact, the practice is older than Christianity. But when Christ came into the world, he revealed the great value of withdrawing for a time from commerce with the visible world to communicate with God and the world of the spirit.

He began his public ministry by spending forty days in the desert. During his three years of preaching, he often left his disciples and the crowd of listeners to go to some quiet place to pray. He would spend whole nights in prayer.

To make a retreat, therefore, is an important practice of our faith and should be part of every devout Catholic's life. We believe that what God became man to teach us, we should imitate. Christ did not need the retreats he made, but we do.

In the sixteenth century, retreats for the faithful of all classes became part of the Catholic Reformation. Led by St. Ignatius, one religious reformer after another promoted retreats among the clergy, religious, and the laity. It was commonly recognized that the breakdown in Catholic unity was mainly the result of interior weakening of faith and moral commitment. The only solution was to strengthen this faith and inner commitment which experience showed could be provided by retreats.

Men like Sts. Charles Borromeo, Francis de Sales, and Vincent de Paul followed the lead of St. Ignatius. As a result, retreats have become part of the ongoing reformation of the Catholic Church.

In making the Spiritual Exercises, it is important to see just what St. Ignatius gave to the rise of the retreat movement. He gave it a definite method, based on the unchangeable principles of Catholic Christianity.

At the heart of this method is an absolute honesty and a selfless charity. I am utterly honest in appraising my spiritual condition. And I am totally selfless in giving myself to Jesus Christ.

All the examinations of conscience, the meditations and contemplations, the vocal and mental prayers of the Spiritual Exercises have this twofold aim: that I may see myself as God sees me, and that I may give myself to him without reserve.

## MEDITATIONS FOR A THIRTY–DAY RETREAT

The meditations in this manual are based on The Spiritual Exercises of St. Ignatius. This means that not only the spirit of the Exercises but their sequence of ideas and their whole approach to the spiritual life is faithfully followed.

As already explained, the Exercises require direction for the retreatant. The direction is partly provided by St. Ignatius himself. But there is further need of guidance on two levels. For want of better words, the two levels may be called objective and subjective. Objectively, those making the retreat should know what meditations they are to make, what the focus of each meditation should be, and how the meditations are interrelated as effective channels of divine grace. The present manual hopes to fulfill this purpose.

Subjectively, each person will need some individual assistance while going through the Exercises. St. Ignatius assumes that this will be available.

## MENTAL AND VOCAL PRAYER

The Spiritual Exercises are a combination of mental and vocal prayer. Mental prayer is that form of prayer in which the sentiments expressed are one's own. Moreover, they are mainly interior and not verbally externalized.

St. Ignatius speaks of two kinds of mental prayer, namely meditation and contemplation. In general, meditation is a reflective consideration of some religious truth. Also in meditation, the mind is more actively engaged in thinking through some mystery of the faith. Contemplation is a loving admiration of the same religious truth, but with the affective powers of the will being more active than the reflective power of the intellect. When I meditate, I am thinking about things in the presence of God. When I contemplate, I am pouring out my heart in loving sentiments towards God.

Vocal prayer is formed in words or equivalent symbols of expression. Also in vocal prayer we use some set formula to express what we have in mind.

In the Exercises, mental and vocal prayer alternate. A single meditation can shift from one form to the other. The important thing is to be aware of God's presence and will to respond to his presence with loving generosity.


## RECOMMENDED PROCEDURE

There is an overall procedure for each meditation that may confuse some people.

Every meditation has a *title* which identifies the content or subject matter for prayerful consideration.

Each meditation is to begin with a *preparatory prayer*. Speaking in the first person, singular, I say, "Lord Jesus Christ, I beg that all the intentions, actions, and operations of this spiritual exercise may tend solely to the praise, reverence and service of thy divine majesty."

After reciting this prayer standing, it is suggested to bow one's head to the floor in adoration of Our Lord.

Depending on the meditation, there will generally be two preludes. The first prelude is a mental representation of the place (as in a Gospel event) or of the subject matter (as when reflecting on some truth of the faith). The second prelude is a petition addressed to God asking for the grace of light or strength that I desire.

During the meditation, or at least before finishing, one or more *colloquies* are made to Our Lord, or the Blessed Virgin. According to St. Ignatius, "The colloquy is made by speaking

*colloquy — conversation or*
*gathering for — theolog discussion*

exactly as one friend speaks to another, or as a servant speaks to a master, now asking for a favor, now blaming himself for some misdeed, now making known his affairs to him and seeking advice in them." Sometimes the words of the colloquy are formulated by St. Ignatius. But generally they are spontaneous expressions of love, sorrow, pleading, or adoration—depending on the focus of the meditation.

A
C
T
S

Following the colloquy and closing the meditation is a recitation of the Our Father or another vocal prayer.

One full hour is the ordinary length of each meditation. There can be more, but normally there are three meditations each day. There can be less than three—even one a day, if necessary. But the efficacy of the Exercises, proved over the centuries, has shown that a generous sacrifice of time to conversing with God is repaid a hundredfold in the bestowal of his grace.

## SPIRITUAL EFFICACY

Among the hundreds of papal commendations of the Spiritual Exercises, the most significant is the encyclical *Mens Nostra* of Pope Pius XI, in which he stated, "We, by our apostolic authority, declare, constitute and proclaim St. Ignatius of Loyola to be the Heavenly Patron of all Spiritual Exercises, and accordingly of all institutes, sodalities or groups, which bestow their care and zeal upon those who are making the Spiritual Exercises."

Without implying the slightest reflection on other retreat methods "which laudably adhere to the principles of sound Catholic asceticism," the pope singled out as the first quality of the Ignatian Exercises "the excellence of their doctrine, which is altogether free from the perils and errors of false mysticism."

Pius XI

Over the centuries, whenever a mystical doctrine departed from the path of orthodoxy it was in one of two directions, either so stressing the operations of grace as to fall into quietism which makes the human will completely passive in the hands of God, or so concentrating on direct inspiration as to remove the need for external guidance from legitimate ecclesiastical authority. The Ignatian Exercises from beginning to end forestall both tendencies by their whole approach to the spiritual life. Their insistence on the autonomous power of human liberty and our capacity for high generosity excludes the danger of ascetical passivism. And their devotion to the Church as the Spouse of Christ and infallible teacher of humanity, concretized in the Rules of Orthodoxy, will not be lost on the most casual retreatant.

The second quality which commends the Exercises is their "admirable facility of being adaptable to any status or condition of men [and women], whether devoted to contemplation in the cloister or leading an active life in the affairs of the world." Historical evidence supports this judgment, that every rank and level of society, in the priesthood, cloister, and the laity, has followed the Exercises with great benefit to personal sanctity and apostolic work. Behind the adaptability was the rare insight that Ignatius had into the basic conflicts and aspirations of our nature, which he derived by going through almost every stage of human experience, from a dissipated youth during which he was once brought to trial for "grave and enormous crimes" to later conversion and spiritual maturity that culminated in the highest form of mysticism.

There is also an "apt coordination of the various parts in the Exercises," and a "marvelously clear order in the meditation of truths that follow naturally one from another." The consequent appeal to the mind is spontaneous, and serves the double purpose of concentrating attention on a single object and integrating different elements in the spiritual life around the focal idea of loving God in the person of Jesus Christ.

But the highest quality of the Exercises is not their freedom from pseudo-mysticism, nor even their logic and adaptability. Their greatest value lies in the power they have "to lead a person through the safe paths of abnegation and the removal of bad habits to the very summit of prayer and divine love."

This is proved experimentally by the changes in moral conduct and spiritual conviction that a single retreat has effected in the lives of thousands of persons. Among the saints, Charles

Borromeo was led by the Exercises "to adopt a more perfect form of life," Francis de Sales "to serve God with the greatest possible fidelity," and Teresa of Ávila to become "the mistress of lofty contemplation." On the level of ordinary piety the experience of every retreat master shows the disproportion, sometimes nearly miraculous, between the time and human effort spent in making the Exercises and the marvelous results they produce. Contributing to this efficacy are many factors that the following pages hope to make clear. But one thing hard to analyze and yet certainly operative is a mysterious element which Pius XI called "a divine instinct." It explains the composition of what some have described as "a book of human destiny," which draws on resources beyond the natural capacity of its author; it may also explain its influence in terms of a supernatural force that God reserves for the chosen instruments of his grace.

# FIRST WEEK

# Introduction to the First Week

WITHIN THE FIRST WEEK OF THE EXERCISES, St. Ignatius includes much more than the basic meditations. He devotes large sections to the daily particular and general examinations of conscience, to Confession and Holy Communion, to the practice of penance and specific directives for making a good retreat.

Even the opening day, on the Principle and Foundation, is more like a prelude to the whole retreat than part of the first week of the Exercises. However, for the sake of simplicity, the thirty days of the retreat will be divided into four weeks, of unequal length.

St. Ignatius believed that dividing the Exercises into four weeks and the weeks into so many days, would provide the exercitant with an organized approach to the spiritual life. This means that the meditations are logically related. Each successive meditation depends on the preceding one. Taken together, they lead to a single purpose: to find out what is God's will for me and, with his grace, to choose what he wants me to do for his greater glory.

In his introduction to the first week, St. Ignatius goes to great length in explaining the General and Particular Examens of Conscience. Not surprisingly, he devotes some 2000 words to this subject after the opening meditation on the Principle and Foundation. The retreatant should carefully read these Ignatian *then* directives on the Examens of Conscience. They are to be put into practice as one of the principal fruits of the Spiritual Exercises.

The two Examens, General and Particular, are not mutually exclusive. They are to complement each other in our pursuit of sanctity.

**General Examen.** This is a daily, or more often, prayerful inventory of my conscience on three levels of reflection.

- *Gratitude.* What graces and blessings, whether pleasant or painful, have I received from God since my last General Examen, for which I will thank him?
- *Sorrow.* What failings did I commit, for which I tell our Lord, I am sorry?
- *Planning.* What do I foresee that God wants me to do in the next day or so? I decide on my agenda and ask our Lord to help me carry it into practice.

**Particular Examen.** Here I concentrate on one particular failing to overcome or a virture to be exercised. Its focus is on such external, bodily or verbal, manifestation of the fault or virtue as can be remembered for periodic inventory. Particular Examens are to be changed weekly, monthly, or otherwise, in order to receive maximum attention. The Particular Examen should also be associated with some brief aspiration or prayerful invocation for divine assistance, the moment a temptation occurs or an opportunity arises for the practice of a given virtue. After some time, another defect to overcome or special virtue to cultivate, is chosen for particular daily examination.

# 1

First Principle *of faith* and Foundation *of morality*

THE PRINCIPLE AND FOUNDATION is a compendium of Christian spirituality. It is the principle of faith from which everything in Christianity finally derives. It is the foundation of morality on which everything in our lives finally depends.

We can distinguish three elementary truths in the Principle and Foundation, to form the master plan of our journey from God the Creator to God as our eternal destiny.

1. • Why are we created?
2. • Why are other things created?
3. • How are we to use creatures to reach heaven?

## 1   WHY ARE WE CREATED?

We are created to know, love, and serve our Creator here on earth in order to reach heaven in a blessed eternity.

We are, therefore, made by God out of nothing. He used nothing and he parted with nothing when he created us. He gained nothing by bringing us into existence and gains nothing by our obedience to his will.

All the benefits of being created are on our side. God wants us to be at peace in this life and perfectly happy in the life to come.

On both counts, peace of soul here on earth and beatitude in eternity depend on our faithful submission to the will of God.

In other words, our eternal future depends on our present behavior. If we sincerely strive to please God here and now, he will reward us by satisfying our fondest desires for happiness in the life that will never end.

### Maxims of St. Ignatius

"How ugly the world is when I gaze upon heaven."

"Lord, what do I desire, what do I desire but you."

"Prefer the glory of God to all things."

| 2 | WHY ARE OTHER THINGS CREATED? |
|---|---|

We exist here on earth to praise (know), reverence (love), and serve God. If we do this, we shall save our souls for heaven and from hell.

This is the end or purpose of our temporal life, that we may reach eternal life in the world to come.

But we cannot reach heaven without using the necessary means of getting there. That is why the rest of the world exists: to enable us to attain our heavenly destiny.

What are these "other things on the face of the earth" that are to help us in attaining the end for which we are created? They are everything that in any way enters or touches our lives. Every person, place, or thing; every pleasure and pain; every circumstance in which we find ourselves; every thought and every desire; every sight we see or sound we hear—are all intended by God to be so many graces leading us to heaven.

There is no such thing as "chance" with God. Everything is part of the loving providence of God, provided by him to enable us to reach him in whom alone our heart can find rest.

St. Ignatius is careful not to use terms like "was created"

either for us or for the world in which we live. He prefers expressions like "*is* created" or "*are* created," to bring out the fact that God's creative power is constantly active in the world and always directed by him as a means of reaching a heavenly eternity.

The secret is to see the hand of God in everything and not make the mistake of thinking that anything merely "happens." With God there is no such thing as fate or fortune or misfortune. All is part of his wise and loving plan for our salvation.

## Maxims of St. Ignatius

"There are few men who realize what God would make of them if they abandoned themselves entirely to his hands, and let themselves be formed by his grace."

"Happy are those who prepare themselves in this life to be judged and saved by his divine majesty. For his love and respect, I ask that, without delay, you most diligently reform your consciences, so that on the day of our final and awesome destiny your souls will be confident."

| 3 | HOW ARE WE TO USE CREATURES TO REACH HEAVEN? |
|---|---|

We are to use the creatures in our lives discriminately and dispassionately. Both adverbs refer to qualities belonging to the essence of our Christian faith.

**Discriminately.** In the words of the Exercises, "We are to use creatures insofar as they help us attain our eternal end, and we are to be rid of them insofar as they prove a hindrance on our road to salvation."

In general, we can distinguish four kinds of creatures in our lives. There are those that God wants us to enjoy. Others he wants us to endure. Still others he wants us to remove. And finally there are creatures he wants us to sacrifice. What does this mean? It means that I must discriminate or separate, classify if you wish, the creatures in my life into four categories and ask myself:

- What persons, places, and things God wants me to enjoy.
- What persons, places or things he wants me to suffer or endure.
- What persons, places or things he wants me to remove from my life because they lead me into sin.
- What persons, places or things in my life are not occasions of sin. But God invites me to surrender them, not because I have to, but because I want to sacrifice out of love for him.

**Dispassionately.** Knowing human nature, Ignatius assumed that we are not spontaneously drawn to what is pleasing to God, nor spontaneously repulsed by what is displeasing to him.

Our fallen nature, tainted by sin and concupiscence, inclines us to what we want and not necessarily to what we need. That is why "we must make ourselves indifferent to all created things, as far as we are allowed free choice and are not under any prohibition." To illustrate what this means we should, consequently, "not prefer health to sickness, riches to poverty, honor to dishonor, a long life to a short life. The same holds for all other things."

This is the bedrock of our struggle through life: "to make ourselves indifferent to all created things," according to the will of God.

This indifference that we are to cultivate is not a denial of the obvious. Pleasant things will remain pleasant, and painful things will stay painful. But we train our wills to control our desires for what is pleasant and our fears of what is painful.

Needless to say, this is not easy. It is humanly impossible, which is why we need the grace of God.

A concluding directive: "Our one desire and choice should be what is more conducive to the end for which we were created."

With the grace of God, we can gradually master our desires. This will enable us to choose what is more certain and more effective in leading us to eternal life.

The comparative "more" is not casual. Our disposition should be to do more than we are obliged to under penalty of sin.

## Maxims of St. Ignatius

"I can love a person in this life only as much as it helps to the service and glory of God."

"Seek the presence of God in all things, in conversation with others, in walking, in looking, in tasting, in hearing, in understanding and in all that we do, since it is a fact that his divine majesty is everywhere by his presence, power, and essence."

# 2

# The History of Sin

STRICTLY SPEAKING, the first week of the Exercises begins with instructions on how to examine one's conscience, even several times daily. There is also a set of directives on General Confession and Holy Communion.

But these are preliminary. The main concern of the first week is with sin. This corresponds to the three points of the first Exercise we are making into three meditations, under the title of, "The History of Sin." This will cover the sin of the angels, of our first parents, and of a person who is condemned to hell for committing one mortal sin.

4  THE SIN OF THE ANGELS

The first sin in created history was that of the angels. Although "they were created in the state of grace... they did not want to make use of the freedom God gave them to reverence and obey their Creator and Lord." Consequently, "falling into pride [they] were changed from grace to hatred of God and cast out of heaven into hell." The purpose of this meditation is to arouse sorrow for sin in the retreatant. I should be "filled with shame and confusion when I compare the one sin of the angels with the many sins I have committed. I will consider that they went to hell for one sin, and the number of times I have deserved to be condemned forever because of my numerous sins."

It is a defined article of the Catholic faith that the demons now in hell were originally in God's friendship. By the abuse of their free will, they condemned themselves to eternal punishment.

We, too, have a free will. In strict justice, we could now be where the fallen angels are except for the mercy of God.

## Maxims of St. Ignatius

"O God, God infinitely good, how do you bear with a sinner such as I am."

"I have never treated of the things of God with a great sinner without finding him better than myself, and without having gained much good for my soul."

"The shortest and almost the only way to achieve sanctity is to have a horror for all which the world loves and embraces."

| 5 | THE SIN OF OUR FIRST PARENTS |

No less than one-third of the angels sinned by their pride, and our first parents followed suit by disobeying God at the dawn of human history.

St. Ignatius emphasizes the dread consequences of the start of original sin. Because of "the sin of Adam and Eve... they did penance for a long time, and... great corruption... came upon the human race that caused so many to be lost in hell."

Not only did the sin of Adam and Eve have tragic consequences on them personally, corruption touched their descendants in many ways:

- Because of the sin of our first parents, we are conceived without the state of grace; this means we had lost the title to heaven.

- Because of their sin, we are deprived of bodily immortality. We are all to die.
- Because of their sin, we no longer have the built-in control of our desires. Without this gift of integrity, we are naturally prone to pride and lust, anger, and greed, envy, sloth, and gluttony.

Having sinned, Adam and Eve "did penance for a long time." Their disobedience will have its consequences on earth until the end of time.

Whatever we learn from this, it should teach us the gravity of sin in the eyes of God. It should also inspire us with a horror of sin as we realize its devastating effects on the human family.

## Maxims of St. Ignatius

"I could never persuade myself that these two things are so combined in any other man as in myself—on my part, to have sinned so much, and on God's part to have received so many blessings from him."

"May it please Our Lady to stand between us, poor sinners, and her Son and Lord. May she obtain for us the grace that in the midst of our sorrows and trials, she may make our cowardly and sad spirits strong and joyous to praise him."

## 6  A PERSON CONDEMNED TO HELL FOR ONE MORTAL SIN

We get some idea of St. Ignatius' awareness of the gravity of sin when he tells us to meditate on a person lost for all eternity "because of one mortal sin." He further says we should "consider also countless others who have been lost for fewer sins than I have committed."

Some have read this passage in the Exercises and put Ignatius down as a renascence fundamentalist. Others have dismissed his view of mortal sin as poetic fancy. But St. Ignatius was no dreamer. His zeal for saving sinners helped to save Western Europe from moral annihilation.

Two elements in this meditation bring out the relevance of Ignatian spirituality: the rising tide of the moral error of the so-called Fundamental Option, and the resurgence of the heresy of Origenism.

Condemned by the Holy See in 1975, the Fundamental Option theory claims that no single crime can be a mortal sin. One abortion, or one adultery is never a mortal sin. It is only when a person becomes so depraved as to totally reject God that we can begin to speak of "a mortally sinful condition."

Origenism, too, is coming back into vogue. The Origenists of the early Church denied either that anyone is permanently in hell, or at least any human beings are punished for eternity. The prevalent idea nowadays is to question whether anyone is certainly in hell.

## Maxim of St. Ignatius

"Nothing should ever be done to lessen the good name of another or to complain about him. For if I reveal a hidden mortal sin of another, I sin mortally; if I reveal a hidden venial sin, I sin venially; if his defect, I manifest my own.

"If, however, my intention is good, there are two ways in which it is permissible to speak about the sin or fault of another:

- When a sin is public, as in the case of a woman openly living a shameless life, or of a sentence passed in court, or of a commonly known error that infests the minds of those with whom we live.
- When a hidden sin is revealed to someone with the intention that he help the one who is in sin to rise from his state. But then there must be some grounds or probable reason for believing that he will be able to help him."

DAY

# 3

# Our Own Personal Sins

IT IS NOT SURPRISING FOR ST. IGNATIUS to be so preoccupied with sin. He had a deep realization not only of the gravity of sin, but the need for each one of us seeing Christ as our own personal Savior.

To this end, it was only logical to make every person aware of his or her own sinfulness.

There are three Exercises on this subject covering a variety of reflections. Among these, the following are chosen for individual meditation:

⟨7⟩ • realization of the gravity of my sins;

⟨8⟩ • understanding of the disorder of my actions in order to really amend my life;

⟨9⟩ • knowledge of the world so that I may put away all that is worldly and vain.

| 7 | A REALIZATION OF THE GRAVITY OF MY SINS |
|---|---|

There is a difference between knowing something and realizing it. St. Ignatius would have us realize the gravity of our past sins.

This means that I "see the loathsomeness and malice which

every mortal sin I have committed has in itself." In a series of statements, I should humble myself by asking two questions:

- What am I, compared with all men and women?
- What are all men and women, compared with the angels and saints of paradise?

Then, considering what all creation is in comparison with God, what am "I alone; what can I be?"

But that is only the beginning. So I continue: "I will consider all the corruption and loathsomeness of my body. I will consider myself as a source of corruption and contagion from which have issued countless sins and evils and the most offensive poison."

Then follow two of the most poignant paragraphs in spiritual literature. They reveal both the insight of a great mystic into the mystery of human depravity and the gratitude of a converted sinner for the unspeakable mercy of God.

> I will consider who God is against whom I have sinned, going through his attributes and comparing them with their contraries in me: his wisdom with my ignorance, his power with my weakness, his justice with my iniquity, his goodness with my wickedness.
>
> This is a cry of wonder accompanied by surging emotion as I pass in review all creatures. How is it that they have permitted me to live, and have sustained me in life? Why have the angels, though they are the sword of God's justice, tolerated me, guarded me, and prayed for me? Why have the saints interceded for me and asked favors for me? And the heavens, sun, moon, stars and the elements, the fruits, birds, fishes, and other animals—why have they all been at my service? How is it that the earth did not open to swallow me up and create new hells in which I should be tormented forever?

As we read this apostrophe of praise of God's mercy, we are moved to pity at the blindness of so many to the horror of sin. And we ask ourselves: How aware am I of the evil I have done by so often adoring my own self-will instead of obeying the almighty will of God?

**Maxims of the Saints**

"The end of sin is death."   St. Basil

"Everyone who commits sin is the slave of sin."   St. Ambrose

| 8 | DISORDER CAUSED BY MY SINFUL ACTIONS |

St. Ignatius tells the retreatant to ask Our Lady, "that she may obtain grace for me from her son... an understanding of the disorder of my actions, that filled with horror of them, I may amend my life and put it in order."

Our faith teaches that every sin has two inevitable consequences: the loss of grace and the incurring of a debt of suffering. Both are disorders brought on by sin.   *We owe some suffering.*

- The loss of divine grace means greater or less deprivation of supernatural life, virtues and merits—caused by sin.
- The debt of suffering is the penalty due for having disobeyed the laws of a just God.

As the author of the Exercises puts it, we are to ask for light to recognize these two disorders which inevitably follow sin. Why? In order to abhor my sinful conduct in the past, amend my life, and practice virtue in the future.

The previous meditation reflected on the horror of sin as an offense against God. The present meditation concentrates on the evil of sin as the cause of terrible harm to myself and others.

Aware of the gravity of our sins, we are to do penance for them. Some bodily penance is always in order. But interior mortification of the mind, will, and emotions is more important.

**Maxims of St. Ignatius**

"Exterior penances are used chiefly for three purposes: first, as a satisfaction for past sins; secondly, in order to overcome oneself, that is to say, in order that sensuality may be obedient to reason, and all that is inferior be more subjected to the superior; thirdly, in order to seek and find some grace or gift which a person wishes and desires; as, for example, if he desires to have an interior sorrow for his sins, or to weep much for them, or for the pains and sufferings which Christ our Lord endured in his passion; or in order to obtain the solution of some doubt he is in."

"We must apply ourselves more fervently in conquering the interior man than the body, in breaking the rebellion of the soul more than the bones."

| 9 | KNOWLEDGE OF THE WORLD TO PUT AWAY ALL THAT IS WORLDLY |

Three times in a single meditation St. Ignatius speaks of the "horror" and "abhorrence" of sin that we should ask for from the Blessed Virgin.

The third time, we are to pray for a knowledge of the world. Why? So that we may be horrified and remove from our lives everything that is "worldly and vain."

Few areas of not only Ignatian but Christian spirituality are more important than a correct understanding of the "world" as found in the New Testament, and especially in St. John.

God created the world (*cosmos*) and saw that it was good. This world, of course, exists. But there is also the world, still *cosmos*, that is in opposition to God and Christ. In this sense, the world is sinful humanity, understood collectively. This world does not recognize either Jesus or the Father (Jn 1:10; 17:25). Indeed, the world hates Jesus (Jn 7:7; 15:18). The world is under judgment (Jn 12:31), as is the ruler of the world (Jn 16:11), who has no power over Jesus (Jn 14:30). Jesus does not pray for the world (Jn 17:9), meaning unredeemed humanity, in every case. Since the world can't be redeemed and reconciled to God on its own, the world ceases to be what it used to be. When the disciples are told not to love the world (1 Jn 2:15), this does not refer to humanity in general but to humanity as the personified hostile power which crucified Christ and opposes his followers.

## Maxims of St. Ignatius

"You say how much evil, how many snares and deceits surround you on all sides. I was not surprised at it, and had it been worse, it would not have astonished me. For as soon as you decide and will to labor with all your strength for the glory, honor and service of God, our Lord, by that very fact you join battle with the world and raise a standard against it."

"The shortest, and almost the only way to achieve sanctity is to have a horror for all which the world loves and embraces."

# 4

# Retribution for Sin

St. Ignatius closes the first week of the Exercises with a meditation on hell. But then he adds the following directive, "If the one giving the Exercises judges that it would be profitable for the retreatant, other Exercises may be added here, for example, on death, and other punishments of sin, on judgment, and so forth."

Our plan here is to have three meditations in the following sequence: death and judgment, purgatory, and hell.

There is retribution for sin already in this life. But the Ignatian emphasis is on the consequences of sin at the end of our mortal life and after our bodily death.

## 10 | DEATH AND JUDGMENT

As Catholic Christianity understands death, it is the cessation of the bodily functions of a human being through the departure of the soul. It is divinely revealed that death is a punishment for sin. According to the church's teaching, death is the consequence of Adam's sin, as declared by St. Paul, "... Sin entered the world through one man, and through sin death..." (Rom 5:12b, JB).

Death is also the end of human probation or testing of one's loyalty to God. It ends all possibility of merit. Strictly speaking, only the body dies. However, the Bible speaks of a second death (Rv 20:6), referring to the souls in hell, who are separated from the principle of supernatural life, which is the indwelling Trinity.

There are two judgments after death. The particular judgment takes place as soon as the soul leaves the body. The general judgment will take place on the last day at the end of the present world.

Note that both judgments refer to either reward or punishment or both. In common usage, however, the judgments are more associated with penalty for sin than with reward for the practice of virtue.

### Maxim of St. Ignatius

"I think that sickness and other temporal losses often come from the hand of God Our Lord so that we may grow in understanding and renounce the love of created things; and so that we may reflect especially on the shortness of life in order that, thinking of eternity, we may adorn our souls."

## 11 | PURGATORY

There is no explicit meditation in the Exercises on purgatory. However, it is implied in St. Ignatius' directives for the examination of conscience, where he speaks of sinning venially if we do not give full consent to a thought or action which is gravely sinful by its nature. He returns to the same theme, in the meditation on the Three Degrees of Humility, where in the second degree, "not for all creation, nor to save my life, would I consent to commit a venial sin."

Among the truths of faith denied by those who broke with the Catholic Church in Ignatius' day was the doctrine of purgatory. The Council of Trent therefore repeated the solemn teaching of the Church on the existence of purgatory and stressed the value of our Masses, prayers, and sacrifices for the poor souls who temporarily reside there.

Meditating on purgatory should make us more clear in seeing the wickedness of sin, even venial or not fully deliberate mortal sin. It should also bring out the suffering due to our sins, even though forgiven. They can be forgiven as to guilt or the restoration of grace, but still require expiation by temporal punishment either here on earth or later after bodily death in purgatory.

A meditation on purgatory should also inspire us to pray and perform good works for the poor souls. We can relieve them of either the length of time in purgatory or of the intensity of their pain.

### Maxims of St. Catherine of Genoa

"When the soul is in sin, God does not cease to urge and inwardly call it. And if it responds to his gentle wooing, he receives it back into his grace with the same love as before, and has no wish to remember that he has ever been abandoned, and never ceases to show it all the benefits he can."

"What a task it is to purge the soul here below and restore her with no further purgatory to her pristine purity... She must pass through many cruel sufferings that she may gain merit by many and grievous penances."

## 12 | HELL

There is one formal meditation on hell in the Spiritual Exercises. It is detailed in the extreme.

To help the retreatant avoid ever sinning mortally again, St. Ignatius offers two preludes to the meditation on hell: imagining what hell is like by a mental representation and asking God for a deep fear of hell.

There are five points covering each of the bodily senses. I picture in my imagination the lost souls "enclosed as it were, in bodies of fire." I hear their "howling cries, and blasphemies against Christ Our Lord and against his saints." I smell "the smoke, the sulphur, the filth, and corruption." I taste the bitterness of "sadness and remorse of conscience." I feel the agonizing pain of the "flames which envelop and burn the souls."

In the colloquy, I am to enter into conversation with Christ and recall why people go to hell. People go to hell either because they refuse to believe or, though believing, refuse to obey the commandments of God.

The basic prayer is to thank the Lord God for allowing me to be still on earth and not suffer the eternal punishment I have deserved for my sins.

## Maxims of the Saints

"If I saw the gates of hell open and I stood on the brink of the abyss, I should not despair, I should not lose hope of mercy 'because I trust in thee my God.'" St. Gemma Galgani

"We must never lose sight of the fact that we are either saints or outcasts, that we must live for heaven or for hell; there is no middle path in this. You either belong wholly to the world or wholly to God. If people would do for God what they do for the world, what a great number of Christians would go to heaven." St. John Vianney

# 5

# The Kingdom of Christ

THE MEDITATION ON THE CALL of Christ the King is by all odds the center of the Catholic apostolate.

It presupposes the whole panorama of divine revelation, going back to the ancient patriarchs and culminating in the coming of Jesus Christ.

Its purpose is to pass from the simple realization of my sinfulness into the supernatural ambition of joining with Christ in the salvation and sanctification of the world.

There are basically three areas of prayerful reflection:

- the power and need of human leadership,
- the call of Christ the King, and
- recognition of Christ as Eternal Lord of all things.

Each of these areas calls for at least one meditation.

Moreover, for the rest of the Exercises, St. Ignatius recommends prayerful reading from the *Imitation of Christ*, the Gospels, and from the lives of the saints.

## 13 THE POWER AND NEED OF HUMAN LEADERSHIP

The modern world with its stress on democracy and individualism may underrate the power and need for personal leadership.

But this very fact only proves the law: people want leaders in human society because they need them.

This is the underlying theme of St. Ignatius' first part of the kingdom meditation on the Call of an Earthly King.

Seven hundred years of defending the Catholic faith in Moorish Spain shaped the Christians of that nation in a way that most people do not realize.

St. Ignatius was born in 1491, the year that Grenada, the last stronghold of Islam in Spain, was finally conquered. Ignatius later became a soldier. His wounding in battle and enforced convalescence were the occasion of his conversion from a life of tepidity and sin to a life of apostolic sanctity.

All of this should be kept in mind in this meditation. As given by Ignatius, its focus is on an earthly monarch who calls his people to follow him in his desire "to conquer all the lands of the infidel." He invites his good subjects to join him in this noble enterprise. Anyone who refuses the invitation should be blamed by the whole world as an ignoble coward.

The lesson for us in our day is stark in its simplicity. The world desperately needs leaders in civil society: persons who have a strong faith in God, a deep sense of mission for the welfare of their citizens, a dynamic zeal to overcome the destroyers of human life and the family, and a magnetic personality that attracts devoted followers.

## Maxim of St. Ignatius

"I am sure that, with the perfect grace and gentleness which his divine majesty has bestowed on your highness for his greater service and praise, your highness will take time to recognize his graces and will be able to distinguish what is good from what is bad, to your own advantage. You will understand that, the more we desire to succeed apart from offense on the part of our neighbor, in clothing ourselves with the living of Christ, Our Lord which is woven out of insult, false witness, and every other kind of injustice, the more we shall advance in spirit and earn those spiritual riches with which, if we are leading spiritual lives our souls are sure to be adorned" (Letter to the King of Portugal, John III, March 15, 1545).

## 14 | THE CALL OF CHRIST THE KING

There are three points to this key meditation of the Exercises. Each level is progressively higher in its willingness to respond to Christ's call.

- On the first level, Christ addresses his potential followers: "It is my will to conquer the whole world and all my enemies, and thus to enter into the glory of my Father. Therefore, whoever wishes to join me in this enterprise must be willing to labor with me, that by following me in suffering, he may follow me in glory."

The motive offered here by Christ is pragmatic. Those who are willing to follow him in labor and suffering are assured the reward of joining with him in his glory.

- On the second level, the prospective followers of Christ are told to think through this royal invitation. If they are of sound judgment, their reason enlightened by faith will tell them: "This is a wise opportunity. We should not only give ourselves to this cause, but give *ourselves entirely.*"
- On the third level, among those who volunteer to join Christ in his mission of conquering the world for his heavenly Father, some wish to go still further. They want "to give greater proof of their love." They want "to distinguish themselves in whatever concerns the service of the eternal King and the Lord of all."

What do they do? They "not only offer themselves entirely for the work but will act against their sensuality and carnal and worldly love, and make offerings of greater value and more importance."

This is the foundation for everything else that follows in the

Spiritual Exercises. As we shall see in the scores of meditations to follow, it is nothing less than "going the whole way." It is love at its highest, the love that seeks to become like the beloved, who having joy set before him, chose the cross.

## Maxim of St. Ignatius

"If God gives you a harvest of trials, it is a sign of the great holiness to which he desires you to attain. Do you want to become a great saint? Ask God to send you many sufferings. The flame of divine love never rises higher than when fed with the wood of the cross, which the infinite charity of the Savior uses to finish his sacrifice. All the pleasures of the world are nothing compared with the sweetness found in the gall and vinegar offered to Jesus Christ; that is, hard and painful things endured for Jesus Christ and with Jesus Christ."

## 15 | ETERNAL LORD OF ALL THINGS

The third and highest level of generosity in giving oneself to follow Christ the King is expressed in the prayer, Eternal Lord of All Things. This prayer is at once an epitome of selfless love of God who became man out of love for us, a compendium of Christian spirituality, and a formula for the Catholic apostolate. Those who say this prayer and live it are the giants of apostolic achievement, as two millennia of the church's evangelization have shown.

It seems best to meditate on this prayer according to the several parts into which it can be logically divided.

**Salutation.** Eternal Lord of all things, in the presence of thy infinite goodness, and of thy glorious mother, and of all the saints of thy heavenly court.

**Offering.** This is the offering of myself which I make with thy favor and help.

**Deliberate choice.** I protest that it is my earnest desire and deliberate choice, provided only it is for thy greater service and praise.

**Commitment.** To imitate thee in bearing all wrongs and all abuse and all poverty, both actual and spiritual, should thy most holy majesty deign to choose and admit me to such a state and way of life.

First I address myself to Jesus Christ by acknowledging him as the Lord of the universe. I further solemnize my prayer by making it in the presence of the Mother of God and of all the saints.

Then I offer myself twice over: It is I who am consciously making the oblation and it is myself whom I am sacrificing.

Moreover, my self-giving is being done from interior conviction and after careful deliberation. I presume that my self-surrender is not just for God's glory. I intend for his *greater* glory that he may be better known and more loved by an ever larger multitude of his rational creatures.

Finally, the commitment I make is to strive to become more like Christ in patiently bearing every kind of injustice (wrongs), every form of abuse (opposition), and every depth of poverty (deprivation). Indeed I offer myself to live this way for the rest of my days on earth.

Whatever my future before eternity may be I hereby make this promise: either to choose a state and way of life or to reform a state and way of life already chosen, where I can carry out my total oblation.

## Maxim of St. Ignatius

"As a recompense, he [Christ] has given us himself, giving himself as a brother in our flesh, as the price of our salvation on the cross, as the food and companion of our pilgrimage in the Eucharist. Ah, how poor a soldier is he who has not been induced to work for the honor of such a prince by such recompense!

"In a certain way, he has deprived himself of the most perfect happiness, of his goods to give them to us, taking upon himself all our miseries to free us from them, desiring to be sold in order to redeem us, dishonored to glorify us, poor to enrich us, suffering death in such ignominies and torments to give us an immortal life of happiness.

"You live in an age when you must show your desires by your works. Look around you: where is the divine majesty honored, where is his tremendous greatness venerated, where is his most holy will obeyed?... See the misery into which souls are plunged.

"What need there is to prepare yourselves for all manner of work and struggle to make of yourselves efficient instruments of divine grace for such a work! Especially when there are so few loyal workers 'who do not seek their own advantage, but that of Jesus Christ.'" **Phil 2:21**

# SECOND WEEK

# Introduction to the Second Week

THE CALL OF CHRIST THE KING is a cameo of the second week of the Exercises.

Since sin entered the world, and God had promised to send a Redeemer, the life and teaching, death and resurrection of Christ are the fulfillment of this promise.

Our lives on earth are to be, as the Fathers of the Church call it, a reduplication of the life of the Savior. What he, the Creator, freely chose to do out of love for us, we are to choose to reduplicate in our lives out of love for him.

This is more than imitating the life and death of Christ. It is even more than just a readiness to follow him. It is nothing less than mysteriously "making up" in our lives what is, dare we say it, "wanting" in the life of Christ. What can possibly be "wanting" in the redemptive work of the Savior? What is wanting, is what God wants, namely our voluntary cooperation with the graces he won for us during his visible stay on earth.

# 6

# The Incarnation

THE INCARNATION IS THE CARDINAL MYSTERY of Christian revelation. It is an event of recorded history. And it is the foundation of everything we hope for in a heavenly eternity.

St. Ignatius' preoccupation with the divinity of Christ is not accidental. It places the humanity of the Son of God in proper focus and gives it a dogmatic foundation without which the following of Christ would be only devotion to a great leader or dedication to a great cause. It would not be the imitation and service of God in human flesh.

Throughout the Exercises, the retreatant learns to know Christ more intimately in order to love him more ardently and in order to serve him more faithfully. The knowledge of Christ, therefore, is the basis of Christian perfection and the measure of all our holiness. We cannot serve with genuine fidelity unless we love, and we cannot love unless we know. But what does it mean to know Christ? What is there to know about him and what kind of knowledge do we have? The answer to these questions cuts so deeply into the science of theology that it separates the whole Christian world into two camps, those who possess the true faith and those who do not. And among true believers, it distinguishes those who live only on the surface of Christianity from those who have penetrated to its depths.

<h2>16     THE WORD WAS MADE FLESH</h2>

Given the liberty that St. Ignatius allows in structuring the Exercises, we shall begin the three meditations on the Incarnation with what he calls a "contemplation on the Incarnation." Our title is from the Gospel of St. John, "The Word was made flesh."

St. Ignatius calls it a contemplation because it opens with a hypothetical scene. But the scene is founded on revealed truth, namely that God chose to become man to redeem humanity from the consequences of its sinful estrangement from God.

The three divine persons are pictured as looking down on the earth and seeing so many people going to hell. So they decide that "the second person should become man to save the human race." The place chosen for the Incarnation is "the city of Nazareth in the province of Galilee."

What do I pray for? "I ask for an intimate knowledge of our Lord, who has become man for me, that I may love him more and follow him more closely."

The points which follow these preludes are viewed in the extreme. They recommend that the one making the retreat reconstruct in the imagination what the persons on earth, the Trinity in heaven, and Our Lady and the angel at Nazareth are doing and saying. Then, says Ignatius, "I shall reflect upon all to draw some fruit from each of these details."

The colloquy is to "beg for grace to follow and imitate more closely Our Lord who has just become man for me."

### Maxim of St. Ignatius

"After God Our Lord had created heaven, earth and all things, and when the first man was in paradise, it was revealed to him how the Son of God had resolved to become man. And after Adam and Eve had sinned, they recognized that God had resolved to become man in order to redeem them from sin... and then they passed this knowledge down to their children, how the Son of God, our creator and Lord, proposed to become man."

**Catechism used by St. Ignatius**

---

| 17 | THE ANNUNCIATION

After citing the full text of the annunciation in the Gospel of St. Luke, the author of the Exercises divides the meditation into three parts. Most of the mysteries in the life of Christ are separated in this way, it may be held, in honor of the Holy Trinity.

- The Archangel Gabriel greets Our Lady with the words, "... Hail, full of grace..." (Lk 1:28b). He tells her she will conceive in her womb and bring forth a Son. He will be called the Son of the Most High.

Thus Mary knew, even before she conceived Jesus, that he is the Son of the living God. She believed in his divinity.

- The angel replies to Mary's question of how this would take place since she was (and was to remain) a virgin. Her kinswoman Elizabeth has miraculously conceived a son in her old age. Thus Our Lady's faith was made credible.
- Thereupon Mary accepted the invitation to become the Mother of God. She calls herself the handmaid, or servant, of the Lord. Her "*fiat mihi*, let it be done to me," was her loving consent. She freely chose to cooperate with the grace of God. On her decision depended the future destiny of the human race.

**St. Robert Bellarmine's Prayer to Our Lady**

Virgin
adorned and clothed with the sun, come to my aid.
most beautiful, Mystical Rose, take abode in my heart.
most chaste, all undefiled, grant me true peace.

deserving of honor and praise, give me your love.
elect and full of grace, lead me to God.
most blessed, Star of the Sea, dispel the storms besetting me.
most virtuous, holy and sweet, guide me on the way.
illustrious, with your burning light enlighten my mind.
more precious than jewels or gold, make reparation for me.
most worthy of all praise, Mother, daughter, and immaculate
    spouse.
and Mother, make me more pleasing to Jesus your Son.
innocent of any stain or fault, make me more worthy of God.
enriched with every gift and grace, obtain the remission of my sins.
most pure, lead me to the joys of heavenly love.
a lily among thorns, I ask you for the grace of a happy death.
more rare than the rarest dream; bring joy to my heart.
so great there is none like you on earth, bring peace to my soul.
most true, loving mother too, Virgin Mary.
Amen.

*Vergine Adorna*

## 18    THE VISITATION

Our Lady's visitation of Elizabeth is the most profound and extensive Marian revelation in sacred Scripture.

It is the most profound because it reveals Mary's divine maternity, her role as mediatrix of divine grace, her sublime faith and selfless charity.

- Elizabeth addressed Mary as "... the mother of my Lord..." (Lk 1:43b).
- When Mary's greeting reached Elizabeth's ears, the infant John the Baptist stirred in his mother's womb. Why? Because at that moment the unborn Christ, through his mother's voice, sanctified the also unborn John, who tradition tells us was born in the state of grace, without original sin.

Elizabeth praised the trusting faith of Mary, "... because the things promised her by the Lord shall be accomplished" (Lk 1:45b). Our trust in God is the principal test of our faith in God. Mary's faith was so firm that her confidence in God's promises was unshakable.

- Mary hastened to help out her aged kinswoman. St. Ambrose tells us that charity is always in a hurry. Once Mary's services were no longer needed, she returned to her home at Nazareth.

The Magnificat of the Blessed Virgin is a retreat all by itself. In the tradition of the great women of the Old Testament— Hannah, Deborah, Judith, and Esther—Mary sings the canticle which over the centuries has become part of the church's liturgy. The lessons of the Magnificat are fundamental to Marian spirituality. Each lesson is a paradox.

- We are to praise (magnify) God before we praise men and women.
- We are to rejoice in doing the will of God before we rejoice in doing our own will.
- We are to be humble if we hope to be blessed by God.
- We have access to the almighty power of God provided we see ourselves as servants of God's name.
- We have the promise of God's mercy if we humbly fear to offend him.
- We can expect God to do great things through the humble and to humiliate the proud.
- We are assured the riches of God's grace if we are hungry to do his will.
- We practice humility when we acknowledge God's gifts to us and put them to use according to his divine will.

## Maxim of St. Ignatius

"May it please Our Lady to intercede with her Son for us poor sinners and obtain this grace for us, that with the cooperation of our own toil and effort she may change our weak and sorry spirits and make them strong and faithful to praise God."

# 7

# The Nativity of Our Lord Jesus Christ

THE HISTORY OF THE HUMAN RACE can be divided into two periods: the centuries from the origin of our first parents up to the coming of Christ, and the two millennia (so far) since the birth of the Savior at Bethlehem.

There is great value, therefore, in seeing at close range the events which surrounded the coming of the Messiah.

Among other possible choices, we shall meditate on the actual birth of Jesus, the visit of the shepherds, and the coming of the Magi.

When we realize that the advent of the Savior was foretold at the dawn of the human family, we should be ready to give our deepest attention to the fulfillment of this prophecy. Not surprisingly, St. Luke provides us with most of the details. Luke was the disciple of Paul, the apostle of converted sinners, who knew the significance of the coming of the Savior of a sin-laden humankind. Luke was also instructed by Our Lady, who of all people would be the most familiar with exactly what happened when her Son was born at Bethlehem. Just for the record, St. Luke is the evangelist of Mary, as he is also the evangelist of divine mercy.

## 19 | THE BIRTH OF JESUS IN BETHLEHEM

St. Ignatius sees three stages in the visible coming of Christ. Each stage is occasioned by circumstances which Mary and Joseph had not planned for. Yet each event that took place had been eternally predestined by God.

**Journey to Bethlehem.** It was the decree of a pagan emperor that brought Mary and Joseph to Bethlehem. Caesar Augustus wanted a census taken of his people, and required each man "...to report to his own town" (Lk 2:3b). Since Joseph was of the family of David, and David's family was from Bethlehem, Joseph took Mary and her child to Bethlehem.

Even as God used the cowardice of the pagan governor, Pilate, to fulfill the prophecy of the Messiah's death in Jerusalem; so he used the pride of the pagan ruler, Augustus, to fulfill the predicted birth of the Messiah in Bethlehem.

**Birth of Jesus.** Christ was born in a stable because "... there was no room for them at the inn" (Lk 2:7b, JB). Once again, God used the humiliating fact of having no respectable and available lodging for his divine Son's birth as man, to teach us what we so desperately need: the practice of poverty.

**Song of the angels.** The contrast between the stable where Christ was born, and the song of the angels at Bethlehem could not have been more startling. What is little in the eyes of men and women is great in the eyes of God. No sooner was Mary's child laid in the trough, from which animals could feed, than God sent "... a multitude of the heavenly host, praising God and singing, 'Glory to God in the highest, and on earth peace to men of good will'" (Lk 2:13b-14).

Two profound mysteries were revealed in the hymn.

- God in the heavens is to be glorified, not only by human beings but by the angels, for his humble birth as a man.

- Peace is promised through Christ to those whose will is good because it is conformed to the will of God.

## Poem of St. John of the Cross

Now that the season was approaching
Of his long-expected birth,
Like a bridegroom from his chamber
He emerged upon our earth

Clinging close to his beloved
Whom He brought along with him.
While the gracious Mary placed them
In a manger damp and dim.

Amongst the animals that round it
At that season stretched their limbs,
Men were singing songs of gladness
And the angels chanting hymns,

To celebrate the wondrous marriage
By whose bond such two were tied,
But the wee God in the manger
He alone made moan and cried;

Tears of man in God alone,
The joy of God in men was seen
Two things so alien to each other,
Or to the rule, had never been.

*The Birth of Christ*

## 20 | THE SHEPHERDS

Again three phases to the role of the shepherds at Bethlehem: they are informed by an angel that the Savior was born that day; they go to Bethlehem with haste, where they found Mary and Joseph, and the infant lying in the manger; they return to glorify and praise God and spread the good news to everyone they could.

**Angelic message.** The message of the angel was the "… good news… (gospel) of great joy…" (Lk 2:10b). There is no joy in the human heart like the happiness that comes from knowing that a person is "at-one" with God. This is the great gift that Christ's coming brought to a sinful world.

**Finding the Christ Child.** This is the second time that Luke refers to people going in haste after an angelic message. Mary hastened to Elizabeth, and the shepherds hastened to find the newborn Jesus.

We are told that, on seeing Christ in the manger, "… they understood what had been told them concerning this child" (Lk 2:17b). The humility and trusting faith of the shepherds enabled them to grasp with their minds the meaning of what they saw with their bodily eyes.

**Glorifying and praising God.** As the evangelist makes plain, the shepherds did not keep this experience to themselves. They were, after the angels, the first apostles of the Word-made-flesh. Later on the twelve apostles were also heralds of the Word of God, in fact, of the Word who is God. Humility and simplicity were characteristics of the shepherds, as they were also of the apostles sent by Christ to proclaim the gospel to the whole world.

### Maxim of St. Bernard

"Poverty was not found in heaven. It abounded on earth, but man does not know its value. The Son of God, therefore, treasured it and came down from heaven to choose it for himself, to make it precious to us."

## 21 | THE MAGI

By way of exception, instead of Luke, it is the evangelist Matthew who gives us the narrative of the visit of the wise men to the infant Jesus.

**The star sends the Magi.** Under divine inspiration, wise men from the Orient were led to find the Christ Child. Where the shepherds represented the chosen people of Israel, the Magi typified the Gentiles. The whole of mankind was to benefit from the Savior's birth at Bethlehem. As explained by St. Augustine, this was no merely natural light which appeared. Moreover, says St. John Chrysostom, "it was not a star at all... but some invisible power transformed into this appearance." When King Herod and his court heard about the star, they were thrown into panic. A rival king, a descendant of David, was born in Bethlehem to "threaten" Herod's petty kingship!

**Worship and gifts.** The evangelist simply says that on reaching "the place," no longer the stable, where Jesus was, the Magi "... falling down... worshiped him...." (Mt 2:11b). Their gifts were deeply symbolic. Thus the church's earliest liturgy declares: "The gold acknowledges him as king, the myrrh declares him to be a man, and the incense proclaims him as God."

**Warning against Herod.** Having paid their respects to the Infant Christ, the Magi were warned in a dream not to return to Herod who wanted to destroy the child. They went back to their own country "... by another route" (Mt 2:12b).

No sooner did the Magi leave than Joseph, too, was warned in a dream to take the child and his mother and "... flee to Egypt..." (Mt 2:13b).

The opposition to Christ, therefore, began almost as soon as he was born. And the root of the opposition remained basically the same up to Calvary. Christ—and his teaching—were seen as a threat to the power and prestige of people whose hearts were intoxicated with the things of this world.


## Maxims of the Saints

"The honors of this world, what are they but puff, and emptiness, and peril of falling." St. Augustine

"The human mind is prone to pride even when not supported by power. How much more, then, does it exalt when it has that support." St. Gregory the Great

# 8

# Presentation in the Temple

THIS DAY IS DEVOTED TO THREE EVENTS in the life of Christ before he began his public ministry.

As far as we know, the flight into Egypt took place after the Lord's presentation in the Temple and Mary's purification. On returning from Egypt, the Holy Family lived at Nazareth, and there is no further record in the Gospels until Christ went to the Temple, where Mary and Joseph found him after three days of searching.

The relative silence of the canonical Gospels about Christ's stay in Egypt and his years at Nazareth is in marked contrast to the apocryphal gospels. There are no less than twenty-one of these apocrypha, allegedly describing the life of Christ during the thirty years from his birth to the beginning of his public ministry.

Consistent with his preference for threes, in honor of the Holy Trinity, St. Ignatius offers three aspects (points) for each of today's meditations.

| 22 | THE PURIFICATION OF OUR LADY AND THE PRESENTATION OF THE CHILD JESUS |
|----|---|

In the church's liturgy, the feast of Our Lady's Purification, according to Mosaic law, is also the feast of the Presentation of the Child Jesus in the Temple. It is also called Candlemas Day, to commemorate Simeon's prophecy that Christ would be "a light to enlighten the pagans..." (Lk 2:32a, JB).

**Purification and presentation.** Both essentials of this mystery are identified by the evangelist: "When the days of her purification were fulfilled according to the law of Moses, they took him up to Jerusalem to present him to the Lord" (Lk 2:22). According to Jewish law, a woman after childbirth was considered unclean and had to keep to herself for forty days if her child was a boy, and eighty days if a girl. Then the mother was to come to the Temple for purification and make an offering which for the poor was fixed at a pair of doves or pigeons. If the child was her first and a boy, then according to the law he belonged to Yahweh. His parents were, therefore, required to "buy him back" by paying five shekels to the Temple.

**Simeon's *Nunc Dimittis*.** As providence would have it, just then a devout man by the name of Simeon was in the Temple. He was assured by the Holy Spirit that he would not die before he had seen the promised Messiah.

Simeon's *Nunc Dimittis*, like Mary's *Magnificat*, is part of the Church's Liturgy of the Hours. His prophecy to Our Lady that "a sword shall pierce your soul..." (Lk 2:35a), was fulfilled to the letter. Her Son's body was pierced with a lance on Calvary. Her soul was pierced with sorrow, not only on Good Friday, but throughout her life on earth. She saw him literally as a sign that was contradicted during his visible stay on earth and foresaw that he would be contradicted in his mystical person, the Church, until the end of time.

**Anna the prophetess.** Also providentially, the aged woman Anna witnessed the presentation. Her years of fasting and prayer were rewarded. She recognized the child as the Redeemer and, like the shepherds, spoke of him to all who were awaiting the Messiah.

**Maxim of St. Alphonsus Ligouri**

"Say always, 'My beloved and despised Redeemer, how sweet it is to suffer for you.' If you embrace all things in life as coming from the hands of God, and even embrace death to fulfill his holy will, assuredly you will die a saint."

## 23 | THE FINDING IN THE TEMPLE

Although the duty to observe the whole law did not begin until a Jewish boy was thirteen, his parents often anticipated the obligation by a year or two. So it was in the case of Jesus.

**From Nazareth to Jerusalem.** His going to the Temple with Mary and Joseph at the age of twelve shows how solicitous he and they were to obey the Mosaic law. No doubt, Christ came to bring the New Law. But he insisted it was not to do away with the Old Law but to bring it to fulfillment.

**Absent for three days.** Christ acts mysteriously. In this case, he deliberately did not inform Mary and Joseph about his plan to stay in Jerusalem. He foresaw they would be worried. But he did this to teach them, and us, a profound lesson. God periodically withdraws the consolation of his presence in order to enable us to grow in virtue by our practice of patience and trust in his providential love.

**First profession of his divinity.** When Mary and Joseph finally found the young Jesus, his mother asked him a logical question. She knew that his absence was deliberate. Yet, as a mother, she wondered, Why? So he told her "... How is it that you sought me? Did you not know that I must be about my Father's business?" (Lk 2:49b).

Both Mary and Jesus used the same word, "Father," but in two very different senses. Mary spoke of "your father," referring to Joseph who was not the natural father of Christ as man, though legally was so reputed. Christ, on the other hand, spoke of "my Father," as the First Person of the Blessed Trinity. In this brief dialogue, Jesus made the first public profession of his divinity. As he would make still more clear later on, "The Father and I are one" (Jn 10:30). They are one in their divine nature although distinct as two persons or individuals.

### Maxim of St. Robert Bellarmine

"The New Testament is filled with evidence of the power and efficacy of the holy name of Jesus... Happy are they who can imitate the blessed Mary in her relation to this holy name, who conceive it in their hearts by salutary desires, give birth to it in works of virtue, and persevere in invoking it to the end of their lives."

## 24 | THE HIDDEN LIFE OF CHRIST

Given the span of time, some thirty years, from Christ's infancy to the beginning of his public life, it must seem strange that we have only the episode of the finding in the Temple recorded in the four evangelists.

Saints and scholars have reflected on this mysterious silence. They agree that it was all part of God's revelation. After all, God is infinite and, therefore, unfathomable by the created mind. It is no wonder then that he would spend so many years in our midst yet remain hidden from the curiosity of the crowd.

We have only a few words in Matthew, saying what happened after the Holy Family returned from Egypt. After instructions from an angel, Joseph took his family to Nazareth.

St. Luke is almost as reticent. But he tells us three things about Jesus that St. Ignatius builds into a meditation. Christ was obedient. He grew in wisdom and age and grace. And he was reputed to be a carpenter.

**Obedience of Christ.** Two thousand years of spiritual genius has built a library of wisdom on the simple statement of St. Luke, "He came to Nazareth, and was subject to them...." (Lk 2:51a). This comes just after Mary and Joseph find Jesus in the Temple after he separated himself from them for three days. During those three days, he was exercising his prerogative as God, to be about his Father's business. During the following years at Nazareth, he was submitting his human will to two human beings to teach us how to obey those who are authorized by God.

**The growth of Jesus.** When God became man, he was truly human, except that he had no sin. As man, therefore, he would be like us in growing up. He certainly grew in age. He allowed himself to grow in grace. And he grew in wisdom in the sense that he acquired knowledge from experience. All the while, however, his human nature was so united with the Godhead that he was one divine person.

**Reputed a mere carpenter.** St. Mark describes what happened when Jesus went to speak in the synagogue at Nazareth. His fellow townspeople were astonished at his wisdom and the miracles he performed. They asked themselves, "Is this not the carpenter, the son of Mary...?" (Mk 6:3a). They were too astounded even to want to believe. As a result, Jesus marvelled because of their unbelief.

## Maxim of St. Ignatius

"He who aims at making, an entire and perfect oblation of himself, in addition to his will must offer his understanding, which is a further and the highest degree of obedience. He must not only will, but he must think the same as the superior, submitting his own judgment to that of the superior, so far as a devout will can bend the understanding."

# 9

# The Two Standards

At this point in the retreat, there is a two-day interval between meditating on the hidden life of Christ and reflecting on his public ministry. Two key meditations intervene, namely the Two Standards and the Three Classes of People.

The Two Standards are a continuation of the Call of Christ the King.

In the Call of Christ the King, he is asking his most devoted followers to give up everything in order to conquer the whole world for the extension of his kingdom.

In the Two Standards, we are brought face to face with a truth of faith: that not only is Christ calling those who believe in him but Satan is also mobilizing those who believe in him.

As might be expected, this is no ordinary day in making the Exercises. It is intended to awaken the retreatant to the realities of life. There are two opposing powers in the world competing for mastery of the human race. Thus St. Ignatius has a set of preludes followed by one meditation each, each for the standard of Satan and for the standard of Christ. We shall make this into three meditations on the three following subjects.

| 25 | THE PRELUDES |

There is a history, a mental representation, and an earnest petition for light from the Holy Spirit—as a person enters on the Two Standards.

**History of conflict.** In an absolute sense, the conflict began when the rebellious angels, led by Lucifer, declared they would not serve the God who created them. They were driven out of their paradise of probation and cast into hell.

Then Satan deceived the parents of the human family. They, too, were driven out of their Eden of probation. But, unlike Lucifer and his followers, Adam and Eve were promised a Redeemer. He came and by his death on the cross broke the stranglehold of Lucifer over humanity. We now have access to such supernatural (which also means supra-demonic) power as our ancestors before Christ only dimly possessed.

**Pictorial representation.** Drawing on the imagery of the book of Revelation, St. Ignatius has us portray the two rival camps: Christ in "the whole region about Jerusalem" and Lucifer around "the region of Babylon."

**Prayer for knowledge and strength.** The great need here is for divine help for the mind to know and for the will to choose. We are, therefore, to pray for discernment of spirits:

- We need to recognize the deceits of the devil and be able to distinguish them from the inspirations of Christ.
- We also need the courage to resist the allurements of Satan and respond to the holy desires coming from Christ.

### Maxim of St. Augustine

"The devil rules over lovers of temporal goods belonging to this temporal world, not because he is lord of this world but because he is ruler of those covetous desires by which we long for all that passes away."

## 26 | THE STANDARD OF SATAN

**The scene in Babylon.** The devils are superb organizers. Their chief is pictured as seated in Babylon "on a great throne of fire and smoke." His real appearance inspires "horror and terror."

**Satanic plot.** Having called together his fellow demons, Satan sends them out to the whole world to seduce human beings away from God. It is a universal mission, "so that no province, no state of life, no individual is overlooked."

**Demonic strategy.** The devils are carefully instructed on how to proceed. Their technique comes in three stages:

- People are first to be tempted to seek or hold on to earthly possessions like money, property, worldly education, and achievement.
- Through these possessions, they are to look for human recognition and honor.
- Thus they are led to pride. Once mastered by pride, they are open to every kind of malice and moral depravity.

### Maxims of the Saints

"When the devil is called the god of this world, it is not because he made it but because we serve him with our worldliness."

**St. Thomas Aquinas**

"Sin it were to believe the devil." **St. Thomas More**

## 27 | THE STANDARD OF CHRIST

**The scene in Jerusalem.** Unlike Satan, Christ is "standing in a lowly place" around "the region of Jerusalem." Also unlike Satan, his real appearance is "beautiful and attractive."

**The vocation and mission.** Christ our Lord does not summon. He rather "chooses so many persons" whom "he sends throughout the world to spread his sacred doctrine among all people, no matter what their state [of life] or condition."

This is the core of the Christian apostolate. Certain people are chosen by Christ. This is their vocation. (Latin *vocatio*, a calling). They are then sent (Latin *missio*, a sending) by Christ to teach and make disciples of all nations.

**Christ's methodology.** How are these apostles of Christ to carry out their mission? The exact contrary to the strategy of Satan.

Satan "goads" his agents "to lay snares for men and bind them with chains." Christ, on the other hand, recommends that his apostles "seek to help all by attracting" them to the three opposites of Satan's conspiracy:

- Drawing people "to the highest spiritual poverty" by internal detachment of the heart from worldly possessions and even further, if it is God's will to give the grace, inviting others to the practice of actual poverty.
- Encouraging people to desire "insults and contempt," in other words, to want—and expect—humiliations.
- Through humiliations leading the followers of Christ to humility and then through humility "to all other virtues."

**Prayer for grace.** Even to seriously intend to follow Christ in this way requires special help from him. That is why St. Ignatius tells the retreatant to first go to "Our Lady, asking her to obtain for me from her Son and Lord the grace to be received under his standard."

## Maxim of St. Ignatius

"We ought to pay close attention. If the devil makes us proud, we must humiliate ourselves by considering our sins and miseries. If he discourages us and casts us down, we must raise ourselves up in true faith and hope in the Lord by recalling to ourselves the good things we have received from him and the great love and will with which he desires our salvation; whereas the enemy cares not whether what he says is true or false but only whether he conquers us."

# 10

# Three Classes of People

By this time in the Exercises, a person has been exposed to enough revealed truth to know that something more is needed. I must look into my own soul to find out where I stand before God.

I know myself too well to have any illusions about my readiness to give up what stands between me and my complete surrender to the will of God.

This obstacle, I may assume, is not of itself sinful. But it is a barrier to my wholehearted surrender to whatever God is asking of me.

How can I react? In one of three ways, depending on my openness to the grace of God.

- I may admit, yes, I have a disorderly affection, but I take no means to overcome it. Then I am a "do-nothing."
- Or I may do something but it is not effective. Then I am a "compromiser."
- Or finally, I may earnestly tackle my self-attachment and take adequate means to reach interior detachment. Then I am an "achiever."

Here, as in the previous Exercise on the Two Standards, I can make three meditations on the one subject, or make the same meditation three times, or—as we are doing—divide the subject into three parts.

## 28 | THE THREE PRELUDES

Given the importance of this Exercise, it is not surprising that there should be three lengthy preludes.

**History of the three classes.** St. Ignatius gives the example of a large sum of money, ten thousand ducats. All three classes of persons have acquired the money honestly. They all want to save their souls. But they are not at peace. Why not? Because they are not interiorly free. They sense that somehow this wealth keeps them from serving God as well as they should.

**In the presence of God and his saints.** Since I am the one with the inordinate attachments, I place myself in spirit before God and his saints. My hope is to discover and choose what is more pleasing to God.

**Prayer for grace.** Faced with a decision that I cannot make on my own, I "beg for the grace to choose what is more for the glory of his divine majesty and the salvation of my soul."

What I am asking is to make the wiser, better, and more generous choice (comparative degree) for glorifying God and reaching my eternal destiny.

### Maxim of St. Francis de Sales

"Self-love is cunning. It pushes and insinuates itself into everything, while making us believe it is not there at all."

## 29 | THE FIRST AND SECOND CLASS

Both these classes have one thing in common. They want to hold on to what their conscience tells them they must be willing to give up.

The only difference between the first and second class is that the first class does not even make a pretense of sincerity. Whereas the second class, consciously or subconsciously, goes through the motions of being freed from the impediment to doing God's will.

The underlying problem is in the mind. We naturally rationalize our motives for doing anything. If I am to be delivered from an obstacle to my spiritual progress, I must first be convinced that something I like *is* de facto an obstacle. Commentators on Ignatian spirituality offer certain signs for recognizing a disorderly attachment even though it is not of itself sinful. Some of these signs are outside of us, and others are deeply internal.

Thus mental preoccupation, frequent attention, habitual admiration, constant distraction, and being the repeated subject of conversation—are all indications that what preoccupies my mind and invariably agitates my will is out of order in my life. I am focused inordinately upon myself or some attachment other than God. So, too, whatever regularly arouses envy or jealousy or anger in me is out of control and needs to be regulated if I am to give my heart entirely to God.

This meditation can, therefore, be a prayerful examination of conscience. As explained by St. Ignatius, I may examine in sequence, my thoughts, words, and actions with one aim in view: to determine where the movements of my soul show I am still enslaved by some of my passions and fears.

## Maxims of the Saints

"We are more troublesome to ourselves than anyone else is to us." St. Francis de Sales

"It is a thing to be especially borne in mind that each individual soul is rendered the more precious in the sight of God in proportion as it is more despised in its own eyes for the love of truth." St. Gregory I

## 30 | THE THIRD CLASS

There are two basic presuppositions for belonging to the third class. I know that I have a disorderly attachment to some creature. I also want to be freed from this disorder. What, then, do I do?

**Readiness to surrender.** I tell God that I am ready to give up the object of my disorderly affection (or fear). The degree of my sincerity with God is a measure of the grace I can expect from him.

**Willingness to do God's will.** Having told God I am ready to give up what I want, I then ask him to make clear to me what *he* wants. Always in view is not merely to avoid sin. It is rather to do what, before God, I believe is "better for the service and praise of the divine majesty."

**Put the willingness to practice.** We are not speculating in this crucial matter. Says Ignatius, "They will strive to conduct themselves as if every attachment to it had been broken." Concretely, this means that I act on my resolution to become internally free.

In other words, I restrain my natural impulse to nourish the inordinate affection. I surrender the natural satisfaction that comes from giving in to what I know is a disorderly inclination in me. As I act this way, God will provide me with the help of his grace. He will give me an increasing supernatural satisfaction that only those can expect who sacrifice their own preferences in order to please God.

### Maxims of St. Ignatius

"No creature can bring the soul such joy as comes from the Holy Spirit."

"The man who has God in his heart carries paradise within him."

"He lives happily who unceasingly, as far as he can, has his mind on God and God in his heart."

## THE PUBLIC LIFE OF CHRIST

St. Ignatius continues the second week of the Exercises with a series of meditations on the public life of Christ. They are placed between the Three Classes of People and the Three Degrees of Humility.

From these reflections on the Savior's public ministry, the retreatant is expected to draw illumination and inspiration:

- The mind is to be enlightened through faith by learning how the Son of God lived during his visible stay on earth; what commandments and counsels he gave his followers; and how he called the apostles and trained them for continuing his saving work until the end of time.

- The will is to be inspired to follow Christ not only passively but actively by joining with him in his mission of redemption. The will is also assured the supernatural strength needed for the apostolate by Christ's promise of grace to those who cooperate with him in the extension of his kingdom.

# 11

# The Baptism and Temptation of Christ

ALL THREE SYNOPTIC EVANGELISTS—Matthew, Mark, and Luke—narrate in detail the baptism and temptation of the Savior. John also begins his Gospel with a discourse on the eternity of the incarnate Word of God, whom John the Baptist proclaimed and who became flesh for our salvation.

Given the prominence of John the Baptist in the New Testament, we shall have three meditations today: the first on John the Baptist himself, the second on his baptizing Jesus, and the third on Christ's temptation by the devil in the desert.

## 31 | ST. JOHN THE BAPTIST

No one, except Christ himself, is given more biographical attention in the Gospels than John the Baptist. John's mission was to prepare the chosen people for the Messiah who had finally come into the world. His message was "Repent, for the kingdom of heaven is close at hand" (Mt 3:2, JB). His language to the stubborn Pharisees and Sadducees was to call them, "Brood of vipers..." (Mt 3:8a, JB). His privilege was to announce to his contemporaries that Jesus was indeed the Lamb of God foretold by the prophets, who was to take away the sins of the world.

We are all, in some way, called to be precursors of Christ. Our own lives of mortification, like John the Baptist's, are to dispose people to repent of their sins and believe in Christ's power to bring them back to a merciful God.

Among the titles given to John the Baptist none is more sobering than, "a voice crying in the wilderness..." (Is 40:3a). John did not succeed in converting the Scribes and Pharisees. In fact, they were mainly responsible for having Christ condemned to death. John did not convert the lecherous King Herod, who had John imprisoned and then beheaded.

John's namesake, the fourth evangelist, describes the precursor as a "man sent from God... to bear witness concerning the light that all might believe through him" (Jn 1:6-7). But what happened? The Redeemer "came unto his own, and his own received him not" (Jn 1:11).

So it was in first-century Palestine. So it has been ever since. There is one consolation, however. To as many as believed in Christ, "... he gave the power of becoming sons of God, to those who believe in his name" (Jn 1:12b). He is doing the same today.

### Maxim of St. Augustine

"A lamp is a creature, not the Creator; and it is lit by participation in an unchangeable light. This was John... He is both light and lamp; nevertheless, compared with the Word... he was not the Light, but was sent to give testimony of the Light."

| 32 | BAPTISM OF CHRIST |

Jesus came to the Jordan to be baptized by John. But John hesitated because he knew this was the innocent Lamb of God. Jesus insisted in order to sanctify the waters of the Sacrament of Baptism and to teach us by his humiliation—as a reputed sinner—that humility is the foundation for reconciliation with God.

It was also on this occasion that the Holy Trinity was audibly and visibly revealed. The Holy Spirit descended on Christ in the form of a dove, and the Father declared, "... This is my beloved Son..." (Mt 3:17b).

There is a close relationship between Christ's humiliation and his exaltation at the baptism in the Jordan. It is a perfect example of what St. Paul meant when he wrote that Jesus "... humbled himself..." (Phil 2:8b). Therefore, "... God has exalted him and has bestowed on him the name that is above every name" (Phil 2:9b).

This is almost the cardinal mystery of Christianity. Our humble acknowledgment of total dependence on God is the precondition for being elevated to an eternal companionship with God. Jesus Christ was true man. He acknowledged his humanity by allowing himself to be baptized as though he were not only human but a sinner. Immediately the Father's voice attested to his divinity.

## Maxim of St. Thomas Aquinas

"Sacraments derive from their institution the power of conferring grace... Now Baptism received this power when Christ was baptized. Consequently, Baptism was truly instituted then if we consider it as a sacrament. But the obligation of receiving this sacrament was proclaimed to mankind after the passion and resurrection."

## 33 | TEMPTATION OF CHRIST

After his baptism among professed sinners, Christ went into the desert "... to be tempted by the devil" (Mt 4:1b). For forty days and forty nights, he fasted to teach us the need for bodily austerity.

Three times the devil tempted the Savior: to gluttony, to presumption, and to idolatrous pride. Each time Jesus countered with a passage from Scripture. Finally he ordered the tempter, "... Be gone, Satan" (Mt 4:10b).

No one is exempt from diabolical temptations, not even the incarnate Lord. The secret is to be alert and resist the evil spirit with courage based on the revealed Word of God.

However, there is a deeper meaning to Christ's temptations by the devil. We cannot say that Christ was tempted as though he could yield to the devil's instigations. He was the infinite God who assumed a human nature. No doubt he had a true human will, with real internal freedom. But he could not abuse this freedom by yielding to temptation. The ability to sin is not a perfection but a liability of human freedom.

What, then, do we mean when we say that Christ was tempted by the devil? We mean two things:

- That he allowed himself to be molested by the evil spirit. It was a painfully humiliating experience.
- That he allowed the devil to test him to find out what the evil spirit suspected but was not sure about. Was Jesus really the Son of God?

What we call "temptations" are not from God's perspective inducements to sin. They are rather trials permitted by him to provide us with the opportunity of proving our loyalty to God.

## Maxims of the Saints

"As the pilot of a vessel is tried in a storm; as the wrestler is tried in the ring; the soldier in the battle, and the hero in adversity, so is the Christian tried in temptation." **St. Basil**

"The demons either tempt us themselves or incite against us people who have no fear of God. They tempt us themselves when we go into seclusion from men, as the Lord was tempted in the wilderness. They tempt through people when we have dealings with them, again as they tempted the Lord through the Pharisees. But if we keep our eyes fixed on our example, that is, the Lord, we shall repulse them alike in each case." **St. Maximus the Confessor**

# 12

# The Apostles, Cana, and the Cleansing of the Temple

AFTER HIS BAPTISM AND TEMPTATION IN THE DESERT, Jesus lost no time in starting his public ministry. Significantly, St. Ignatius chooses three events to highlight this opening of Christ's public life:

- The call of the apostles, which the author of the Exercises carefully points out is recorded by all four evangelists.
- The first miracle performed by Christ at the marriage feast of Cana.
- The cleansing of the Temple when Christ drove the money changers from its sacred precincts.

## 34 | THE CALL OF THE APOSTLES

As mentioned earlier, the apostles were called so that they might be sent by Christ to proclaim the gospel to all the world.

In theological language, a vocation is the special grace that God gives certain people to enable them to carry out the mission to which they are to be sent.

In this sense, the twelve men chosen by Christ to be his closest friends were apostles in the deepest and primary sense. They were *the* chosen men, who were trained to be *the* foundation of the Church for proclaiming *the* message of salvation to the whole human race.

Some of the apostles were called more than once. Thus "St. Peter and St. Andrew seem to have been called three times." There was an initial invitation; then a call to follow the Master, but still with the prospect of returning to their possessions; and finally the vocation to follow Christ forever.

St. Peter is unique. He not only went through several stages of being called. He sinned by denying that he even knew Christ. Then, as recorded by St. John, after being allowed to expiate his triple denial by a triple protestation of love, Jesus finally told him, "… Follow me" (Jn 21:19b).

St. Ignatius points out certain striking features about the apostles:

- They were uneducated men and came from a humble condition of life.
- They were called gently to their exalted dignity.
- They were given such gifts and graces as none of the Fathers of the Old and New Testaments were privileged to receive.

Here again we see the divine consistency expressed by Mary in the Magnificat that God exalts the lowly.

### Maxims of St. Ignatius

"Let the apostolic man not forget himself. He has not come to handle gold but mind. He cannot, therefore, watch himself too carefully that he may not contract the leprosy of which he seeks to cure others."

"There is nothing of which apostolic men have more need than interior recollection."

## 35 | THE MIRACLE AT CANA

In John's Gospel, the miracle at Cana in Galilee follows immediately after the call of the apostles. What happened at Cana was the beginning of Christ's miracles by which he confirmed the faith of his disciples.

**Invitation to the marriage feast.** Jesus had just assembled his first apostles, when his mother was to attend a wedding in nearby Cana. So he and the disciples also came. From all appearances, if Mary had not been there, her Son and his followers would not have been invited.

**Mary's directives.** Whatever the reason why the wedding celebration ran out of wine, it was Mary who noticed it and told her Son, "... They have no wine" (Jn 2:3b, JB). Her solicitude over what may seem a trivial matter reveals the sensitivity of her charity. Christ did not rebuke her. He knew what he was going to do and so he said, "... My hour has not come yet come" (Jn 2:4b, JB). She told the servants. "... Do whatever he tells you" (Jn 2:5b, JB). They followed her instructions. When Jesus told them to fill six large jars with water, they did so.

**The miracle and its consequences.** Jesus then told the attendants to bring the jars to the steward. He tasted what had been water and discovered it was now choice wine. In the evangelist's words, this was the "... first of the signs... and his disciples believed in him" (Jn 2:11b, JB).

Throughout his public life, Christ worked many miracles. While their immediate motive, as at Cana, was to perform an act of charity, their ultimate purpose was to provide rational grounds for the credibility of the Christian faith.

Miracles not only were but are necessary today in order to validate the truth of what we believe. Mary's role as mediatrix of miracles began at Cana. It has continued ever since. And its function is the same, so that his disciples might believe in him and obey him in all things.

**Prayer of St. Aloysius**

"Holy Mary, my Queen, I recommend myself to your blessed protection and special keeping and to the bosom of your mercy, today and every day and at the hour of my death. My soul and my body I recommend to you. I entrust to you my hope and consolation, my distress and my misery, my life and its termination. Through your most holy intercession and through your merits may all my actions be directed to your will and that of your Son. Amen."

## 36 | CLEANSING OF THE TEMPLE

The Gospels not only reveal who Jesus was but also how he reacted to the evils of his day. Then, as now, greed was a passion that infected also those who were the custodians of the house of God.

Right after describing the miracle at Cana, the evangelist says that because the Passover was near at hand, Jesus and his disciples went to the Temple in Jerusalem to pray. Hoping to make extra money on the Passover pilgrims, the Temple was filled with merchants selling oxen, sheep, and doves for use in the ritual sacrifices. The tables were piled high with coins from the exorbitant prices charged the pilgrims.

Jesus saw this. So he made a kind of whip of cords, overturned the business tables and "... drove them all out of the Temple..." (Jn 2:15b, JB). Ignatius notes that "to the poor vendors of doves he said kindly, 'Take these away! Make not the house of my Father a house of traffic'" (Jn 2:16b).

It was deeply providential that the most dramatic manifestation of anger was made by Christ over the profanation of the Temple. At the heart of the wisdom of the world which he castigated is the love of money. In cleansing the Temple of its money changers, Jesus was teaching us what we most need to learn, that we cannot serve God and mammon, where mammon is the riches of this world.

## Maxims of St. Ignatius

"What would be a miracle would be for God to leave unaided those who trust in him. Let us occupy ourselves with the service of God, and leave to him the care of providing for our needs."

"In the hands of God I find what is lacking to me in the hands of men. And if they give me nothing, I shall find all things in him."

# 13

# First Principle and Foundation

## I. The Beatitudes

THE EIGHT BEATITUDES are the Decalogue of the New Law. What the Ten Commandments were to the chosen people of Israel, the Beatitudes are to the people of God in Christianity.

St. Ignatius gives only the Beatitudes, as found in the Gospel of Matthew. They are complemented by the Gospel of Luke, where we find four blessings and four woes or maledictions for those who refuse to follow the Beatitudes.

In today's three meditations, we shall first look at the Beatitudes as a whole, then spend one meditation each on the first four and the second four of the Beatitudes in more detail.

| 37 | THE BEATITUDES AS A VOCATION TO DISCIPLESHIP |

St. Ignatius makes it plain that Christ "proposes the eight Beatitudes to his beloved disciples apart." Or as the evangelist puts it, "Seeing the crowds, he went up the mountain. And when he was seated his disciples came to him. And opening his mouth, he taught them" the Beatitudes (Mt 5:1-2).

What are the Beatitudes? They are eight promises of happiness to those who fulfill eight conditions as followers of Christ.

In the original inspired text, each Beatitude begins with the promise of "Blessed." This means more than merely "Happy." How so? Blessedness is supernatural happiness. It is the fount of grace, and not only a benefit of nature. To be blessed, passive voice, is to be made happy by God, superhumanly happy, as only he can reward those who serve him with their whole heart.

Jesus assured his followers that they would be happy, not only in the life to come, but already here on earth. There is only one proviso: that they conform their wills not only to God as known from reason or revealed in the Old Testament but as both taught and practiced by the incarnate Son of God, Jesus Christ.

Christ's selective proclamation of the Beatitudes to his disciples brings to light an essential aspect of our faith. There is an absolute sense in which the Beatitudes are meant for every Christian believer—but not directly. The disciples were the immediate recipients of the Beatitudes. This was part of their apostolic vocation. But they, in turn, were to live and teach the Beatitudes to others.

That is why after giving them the Beatitudes, Christ proceeded to tell the disciples that they were the salt of the earth and the light of the world.

This, in fact, is the whole genius of Catholic Christianity. Within the Church are those who are spiritually gifted by grace to learn the truths proclaimed by Christ, put these truths into practice, and then proclaim these lived truths to others.

To be stressed is that Christ himself lived the Beatitudes which he proclaimed. Consequently, a good synonym for the imitation of Christ is the practice of the Beatitudes.

The Spiritual Exercises are a proved method of living the Beatitudes with their divinely assured promise of spiritual joy.

## Maxims of St. Ignatius

"No creature can bring the soul such joy as comes from the Holy Spirit."

"Those who carry God in their hearts carry paradise within them."

"There is nothing sweeter than to love God. But the greatest sign of love is to suffer for what one loves. To suffer for God, therefore, is true joy. It is supreme felicity."

## 38 | POVERTY, MEEKNESS, MOURNING, HUNGER, AND THIRST

Each of the Beatitudes sets down the condition for the joy that Christ promises his followers. Each condition is contrary to the wisdom of this world.

**Poverty of spirit.** In the first Beatitude, Christ promises the kingdom of Heaven to those who are internally detached from the things of earth. Heaven and earth are a revealed contrast. The more our hearts are freed from worldly riches and possessions, the more happy we shall be even this side of eternity.

So true is this that, with St. Augustine, we can say that heaven is where the experience of God's presence is enjoyed. We are to enjoy this presence even now in the measure that our wills are conformed with his divine will.

*temperance*

**Meekness.** There is a difference between "meekness" and "gentleness," and both terms accurately express the second Beatitude.

*charity*

Meekness is the virtue of temperance, which controls our natural impulse to anger under provocation. Gentleness is the virtue of charity which restrains our natural urge to severity with those who provoke us.

The promise of Our Lord that we shall possess the earth is not a poetic phrase. It is the assurance of influence, of converting sinners, and of being a channel of grace to others in the degree that we are meek and gentle with them.

**Mourning.** Christ gave us the model for legitimate sorrow when he wept over Jerusalem and at the grave of Lazarus whom he loved. To mourn is to be human as shown by God himself who became the Man of Sorrows.

What is the promise? It is strength of will not only to mourn with patience but to grow in love, because faith tells us we are most pleasing to God when we are most like his divine Son.

**Hunger and thirst satisfied.** The clearest biblical synonyms for strong desire are hunger and thirst. We are told that our desires will be satisfied, even in this life, provided we desire what God wants. What, then, is the secret of happiness, even here and now? It is to know what God wants of us, to choose what he wants, and then to do it. All unhappiness is unsatisfied desire. We are not to be unhappy. And we shall be happy, even this side of heaven, in the measure that we desire what is right—which means what conforms to the loving but often demanding will of God.

### Maxim of St. Ignatius

"Few souls understand what God would effect in them if they should give themselves entirely into his hands and allow his grace to act."

| 39 | MERCY, PURITY, PEACE, AND PERSECUTION |
|----|---------------------------------------|

Throughout the Gospels we find one teaching of Christ after another explaining and illustrating the Beatitudes.

**Mercy as a condition for mercy.** If there is one truth that Christ made plain it is the cause-and-effect relationship between our mercy to others and God's mercy to us.

On reflection this is only as we might expect. God has a profoundly wise reason for allowing us to be offended by others. It provides us with a shower of opportunities to do penance not only for our own sins but also for the sins of others—especially of those who offend us.

**Purity of heart.** Two kinds of purity of heart are implied in this Beatitude. They are purity from sin, or sinlessness; and the purity of chastity. On both counts, the reward is overwhelming: We shall see God. Only the sinless and the chaste of heart have a right to the Beatific Vision of the all-holy God.

But even here on earth, we may speak of seeing God by faith, as the foundation for our hope and love. We are to grow in faith, and the divinely ordained means of this growth are sinlessness and chastity. As we become less sinful, the eyes of our mind perceive God's presence more clearly and deeply. As we grow in chastity, which means chastity of mind and body, our perception of God becomes more vivid and our seeing him, more profound.

**Peacemaking and intimacy with God.** Peace is the absence of conflict. It is the tranquility of order. Immediately, we must distinguish peace of mind from peace of heart. Peace of mind is the experience of knowing the truth. Peace of heart is the experience of doing God's will. There can be no peace of heart unless there is first peace of mind. I must know the truth before I can choose the true good, which is what God wants me to do.

However, there is not only peace within people which makes them peaceful. There is also to be peace between people making them peaceable. Now a crucial statement: There can be no real peace between people unless there is peace within people.

All the discord and all the conflict between people can be traced to a greater or lesser lack of interior peace within those who are in conflict with each other.

Christ's beatitude builds on these premises of Christian spirituality. We are to be peacemakers on three levels.

- We are to help others know the truth. This will bring them peace of mind.
- We are to help others conform their wills to God's will for them. This will produce peace of heart.
- We are to help reconcile people who are in conflict because they are not personally at peace within their own minds and hearts. Our success as reconcilers will finally depend on the grace of God. But it will also depend on our own peace of soul to make us channels of the peace of Christ to others.

The reward for peacemaking is mysterious. It is the promise of a special intimacy with God, like that of children with their parents. God is the supreme Father and Provider of the human race. Our efforts to bring peace to others entitles us to cherish him and be cherished by him with a fondness that only experience can explain.

**Joy in persecution.** The eighth Beatitude has been called a summary of the Gospels. It synthesizes the whole teaching of the Master on following him faithfully even though it necessarily means misunderstanding, rejection, and even persecution from the world that crucified the Savior.

The important word here is "necessarily." When God became human and proclaimed his message of salvation, he was—to put it mildly—not received favorably by those whom he came into the world to save.

Time and again, he repeated that "… a servant is not greater than his master…" (Jn 13:16b; 15:20b, JB). His contemporaries did to him what the contemporaries of his followers would do to those who sincerely strive to become like him. No wonder the promised reward is heaven in the life to come.

There is such a thing as happiness in hope. After all, hope is the confident desire of obtaining some future good. Can there be greater confidence than trust in Christ, the Truth-become-man? Is there any greater good than heaven? Of course, the joys of heaven are in the future for us. But they can be experienced by anticipation already.

## Maxim of St. Ignatius

"Experience usually teaches that there will be greater profit where there are more contradictions."

# 14

# Sermon on the Mount

### II. Patience, Chastity, and Charity

AFTER GIVING THE BEATITUDES, Christ went on to explain how the New Law, which he was proclaiming, went far beyond the Old Law given to Moses and the prophets.

He concentrated on three virtues that would distinguish his followers for all the ages of future history. They were patience, chastity, and charity.

He also made it clear that he had not come to destroy the law or the prophets. Rather he came to fulfill, or complete, or bring to perfection the moral code of Judaism. In each case, therefore, he compared the moral expectations of the Old Testament with the spiritual requirements of the New.

## 40 PATIENCE OF THE HEART

In the Decalogue, the fifth commandment declares, "You shall not kill" (Ex 20:13). The deliberate killing of an innocent person is murder. And the penalty for murder was, and is, capital punishment which is sanctioned by both Testaments of sacred Scripture.

What does Christ do to the fifth commandment? He says that "... everyone who grows angry with his brother shall be liable to judgment..." (Mt 5:22b), according to the measure of his anger. He condemns even the indulgence of an interior movement of animosity, and certainly any spoken words of insult.

Patience is a form of the moral virtue of fortitude. It enables a person not only to refrain from retaliating for an injury. It enables us to endure pain—especially when caused by someone else—and endure the pain without sadness or resentment. How is that possible? It is possible only on the premises of the Christian faith.

We believe that everything is part of the providence of God. We further believe that the pain which others cause us is intended by God for our own purification and sanctification as well as for the spiritual benefit of others, including those who are, heavenly speaking, responsible for our pain.

## Maxims of the Saints

"Patient endurance is the perfection of charity." **St. Ambrose**

"St. Francis de Sales, that great saint, would leave off writing with the letter of a word half-formed in order to reply to an interruption." **St. John Vianney**

## 41  CHRISTIAN CHASTITY

No single area of Christ's teaching has been a greater inspiration to his followers or aroused greater opposition from his critics than his doctrine on chastity.

In the Sermon on the Mount, this comes in two stages. Both deserve to be quoted in full:

### Chastity of Mind and Body

You have heard that it was said to the ancients, "You shall not commit adultery." But I say to you that anyone who so much as looks with lust at a woman has already committed adultery with her in his heart.

So if your right eye is an occasion of sin to you, pluck it out and cast it from you; for it is better for you that one of your members should perish than that your whole body should be thrown into hell. And if your right hand is an occasion of sin for you, cut it off and cast it from you: for it is better for you that one of your members should be lost than that your whole body should go into hell. Mt 5:27-30

### Monogamy in Marriage

It was said, moreover, "Whoever puts away his wife, let him give her a written notice of dismissal." But I say to you that everyone who puts away his wife, save on account of immorality, causes her to commit adultery; and he who marries a woman who has been put away commits adultery.

Mt 5:31-32

What is Christ saying? He is saying that not only are external sins against chastity forbidden but even unchaste thoughts and desires. Behind this momentous elevation of Mosaic law was the authority of the One who was conceived of a virgin mother, lived a life of inviolate virginity, and instituted the sacraments to make Christian chastity not only possible but, for two millennia, a witness to the power of divine grace over the passions of fallen human nature.

What else is Christ saying? He is saying that marital chastity, just as marital fidelity, is also part of the New Testament. He restored monogamy to human civilization and forbade married people to divorce and remarry. Even infidelity on the part of one spouse does not allow the innocent party—who may separate—to enter into another marriage.

The Church founded by Christ has paid dearly in departures from Catholic unity for her uncompromising adherence to Christ's teaching. What is this teaching? That no authority on earth, whether civil or ecclesiastical, can dissolve a marriage in which both partners were baptized before matrimony, had entered into a valid contract in marrying, and consummated their union by natural intercourse after marriage.

## Maxims of the Saints

"Do not say you have chaste minds if you have unchaste eyes, because an unchaste eye is the messenger of an unchaste heart... Lust served becomes a custom, and a custom not resisted becomes a necessity." **St. Augustine**

"A man who governs his passions is master of the world. We must either command them or be enslaved by them. It is better to be a hammer than an anvil." **St. Dominic**

## 42 | CHRISTIAN CHARITY

Throughout the Gospels, especially in Sts. Luke and John, Christ reveals what he called, "The New Commandment."

In the Sermon on the Mount, he concentrates on the one aspect of charity that is most demanding of selfish human nature. He insists on the love of our enemies. His injunction comes in three parts: love your enemies, do good to those who hate you, pray for those who persecute and calumniate you. Each of these three commands brings out the superiority of Christian charity over even the highest form of Mosaic altruism.

**Love your enemies.** By definition an enemy is one who does not love us. By all the laws of natural psychology, we can only love in return for being loved. But Christ enables us to love someone without either having been first loved by that person or expecting to be loved in return.

The grounds for this love of the unloving are found in our faith. We believe that God loved us before we even existed to be able to love him. We also believe that he loves us without his benefitting from that love of his. We finally believe that he became man to redeem us from the tragic consequences of our failure to love him.

**Do good to those who hate you.** This goes beyond the preceding. Christian charity goes beyond not being vindictive, it is, in fact, positively zealous to benefit those who positively hate us. We might almost say it is inventive to find ways of pleasing those who are openly hostile to us.

Again the foundation for this generosity is the mercy of God to sinners and the example of Christ the Redeemer. Nothing so deeply manifests God's love for men and women than his lavish benevolence toward those who have abused his gifts by their sins.

**Pray for those who persecute and calumniate you.** It is not surprising that Christ should tell us to pray for our persecutors and calumniators. Why? Because the greatest good we can do for anyone is to obtain divine grace for a person. Prayer is the most powerful source of grace at our disposal. To pray for someone, therefore, is to become that person's greatest benefactor. Our prayer is the door to supernatural blessing that we are asking God to bestow on the one for whom we are praying.

The marvel is that Christ tells us, in effect, to specialize in our prayers. Of course, we are to pray for our friends, for those who are well disposed to us, for strangers we have never met, and for persons who will never physically enter our lives here on earth. Granted. But we are, Christ says, to be sure to include in our prayerful petitions the persons who oppose us and seek to destroy our good name.

It is not even necessary that we know who these persecutors are, to pray for them. It is certainly not necessary to feel any satisfying emotions as a result. It is only necessary that our wills are fixed in wanting to benefit those who, it seems, are determined to harm us.

### Maxims of the Saints

"He has as yet no perfect love, whose dispositions towards men depends on what they are like, loving one and hating another for this or that, or sometimes loving and sometimes hating one and the same man for the same reasons.

"As memory of fire does not warm the body, so faith without love does not produce the light of knowledge in the soul.

"Whoever entertains in his heart any trace of hatred for anyone, regardless of what the offense may have been, is a complete
stranger to the love God." **St. Maximus the Confessor**

"If you truly want to help the soul of your neighbor, you should
approach God first with all your heart. Ask him simply to fill you
with charity, the greatest of all virtues; with it you can accomplish what you desire." **St. Vincent Ferrer**

# 15

# Sermon on the Mount

### III. The Lord's Prayer (Part One)

THE OUR FATHER OR THE LORD'S PRAYER is the most famous prayer in the world. It is said by more people and has been explained by more commentators than any other verbal form of worship in human history. It is also the one prayer which Christ himself taught his first disciples and, ever since, his faithful followers throughout the ages.

In the Spiritual Exercises, the Our Father is the one prayer that St. Ignatius most often recommends. Moreover, in his Second Method of Prayer he gives explicit directives on how to use the Our Father as the basis for meditation. While kneeling or sitting, as best suits one's devotion, and while keeping the eyes closed or fixing them in one position without permitting them to roam, let the retreatant say, "Father," and then continue "meditating on this word as long as he finds various meanings, comparisons, relish, and consolation in the consideration of it. The same method should be followed with each word of the Our Father." Spending one day on the Lord's Prayer, we shall divide its seven petitions into three meditations. All the while we should remember that the more deeply we understand the meaning of Christ's words, the more glory we are giving to his divine majesty and the more graces we are meriting for ourselves and others.

## 43 | OUR FATHER

As we begin the Our Father, we try to realize to whom we are speaking. It is to all three persons of the Blessed Trinity. We address God as our Father by all the titles of nature and grace.

- He is our Father as the Creator who made us out of nothing, out of sheer selfless love, and with no necessity on his part.
- He is our Father who sustains us in existence and provides for all our needs.
- He is our Father because he made us to his own image and likeness with an intellect and a free will. He is also our Father because he raised us by his grace to share in his own divine life.
- He is our Father because we are destined to possess him in the beatific vision as the heirs of his infinite bounty.

Throughout the Our Father we are speaking to God as social beings. It is *we* and *our* and *us* that runs as a theme throughout, to remind us that our human society is a created reflection of the divine society of the Father, Son, and Holy Spirit.

In addressing God as "in heaven" we are certainly speaking to him in his heavenly glory surrounded by the angels and the saints. But we also know that he dwells in the depths of our souls which, in a sense, is heaven by anticipation. As St. Augustine says, "Heaven is where the presence of God is consciously enjoyed."

### Maxim of St. Augustine

"Observe two kinds of men: the one of those who labor, the other of those among whom they labor; the one of men thinking of earth, the other of men thinking of heaven; the one of those whose hearts are set on the depths, the other of men who join their hearts to the angels; the one trusting in earthly things with which the world abounds, the other confiding in heavenly things, which God, who does not lie, has promised."

## 44 | HALLOWED BE THY NAME

The Latin translation, *"santificetor nomen tuum"* (may your name be sanctified) is more clear than the common English translation, "hallowed be thy name."

What are we asking for in this first petition? We are asking for several things:

- That God may be known by those who do not believe in him.
- That God may be loved by those who are immersed in the love of creatures, and especially themselves.
- That God may be faithfully served by his rational creatures, by their submission to his will.
- That the name of God may be reverently used in prayer and not profaned or blasphemed.
- In a word, that the first and second commandments of the Decalogue may be obeyed.

We pray that the worship of modern idols may cease and that the one true God may be honored by human beings as the first condition for attaining their eternal destiny.

If there is one thing we should pray for in this petition, it is for the recovery of the sacred in all its forms. The sacred is what belongs to God, has been made by God, is seen as the property of God, and revered for the honor of God. Every aspect of the modern world has suffered from a profanation of the sacred. We, therefore, beg God to enlighten modern people that their first duty on earth is to recognize the presence of God and respond to this presence in prayerful dependence on God.

**Maxim of St. Francis de Sales**

"Provided that God be glorified, we must not care by whom."

| 45 | THY KINGDOM COME |

When we pray that the kingdom of God may come, we are asking for many things. The biblical word for "kingdom" is *basilea*, and is the term Jesus normally used when he spoke of his Church.

He laid the foundations for the Church by his incarnation. He prepared the leaders of the Church by his calling and training the apostles. He gave them the authority and power needed by the Church, when he ordained the apostles on Holy Thursday night. The Church was actually born on Good Friday when Jesus died on the cross. And the Church began to propagate and spread throughout the world on Pentecost Sunday.

But so much still needs to be done. That is why we ask God for his kingdom to come. What are we praying for?

- That the millions of non-Christians may have the gospel preached to them and come to believe in Jesus Christ and him crucified.
- That Christians who are not united with the bishop of Rome may once more profess the fullness of the Christian faith in union with the successor of St. Peter.
- That Catholics everywhere may grow in their loyalty to Christ and his teaching.
- That those who belong to the holy Catholic Church may be zealous in sharing their precious treasure with others.
- That the souls in purgatory may soon enter the kingdom of heaven.
- That all of us in the Church Militant (the Church on the earth) may one day be reunited in the Church Triumphant in a heavenly eternity.

## Maxims of the Saints

"The Christian prays in every situation, in his walks for recreation, in his dealings with others, in silence, in reading, in all rational pursuits." **St. Clement of Alexandria**

"When we stand praying... we ought to be earnest with our whole heart. Let all worldly thoughts pass away, nor let the soul think on anything except the object of our prayers." St. Cyprian

"For me, prayer means launching out of the heart toward God; a cry of grateful love from the crest of joy or the trough of despair; it is a vast, supernatural force that opens out my heart and binds me close to Jesus." St. Thérèse of Lisieux

"Reflect what great happiness is bestowed upon you, namely to converse in your prayers with God, to join in colloquy with Christ, and to beg for what you desire." St. John Chrysostom

"The air which we breathe, the bread which we eat, the heart which throbs in our bosoms, are not more necessary for man that he may live as a human being than is prayer for the Christian that he may live as a Christian." St. John Eudes

# 16

# Sermon on the Mount

## IV. The Lord's Prayer (Part Two)

THE LAST FIVE PETITIONS OF THE LORD'S PRAYER are so many requests for divine assistance. Each request has its own identifiable purpose, and yet the five together form a remarkable unity. It is the unity of recognizing our desperate human needs and pleading with the Almighty to answer these needs for his glory and for our salvation.

| 46 | THY WILL BE DONE ON EARTH AS IT IS IN HEAVEN |

In this petition we recognize our free will. We also recognize the free will of God. We finally recognize that we have only one duty on earth, and that is to recognize and choose to do the will of God.

But why the strange comparison? We ask that the will of God may be done on earth by us mortals as it is done in heaven by the immortal angels and saints.

Clearly there is a presupposition. We presume that not all people on earth are doing the will of God. We further presume that they should be doing his will. But why not? One reason is because our freedom is the awful power we have to resist the will of omnipotence. Another reason is that we constantly need the help of God's grace to know what God wants of us and to choose accordingly.

This is the focus here. We are asking God for the light and courage to conform our wills to his according to his designs on our behalf.

We return to the comparison expressed in the petition. What exactly are we praying for? We are praying that, with his help, we may daily come closer to doing God's will now on earth as the blessed are doing in heaven.

- In heaven everyone is doing the will of God.
- In heaven everyone enjoys doing what God wants.
- In heaven everyone is doing the will of the Holy Trinity generously, selflessly, cooperatively, constantly, without envy or jealousy, and with total sincerity.

Certainly we include ourselves in this plea. We know how passionately wedded we are to our own wills and what grace we need to find a foretaste of heaven here on earth.

**Maxim of St. Augustine**

"It is certain that we keep the commandments if we so will; but because the will is prepared by the Lord, we must ask him for such a force of will as enables us to make an act of willing. It is certain that it is we who will when we will, but it is he who enables us to will what is good."

 GIVE US THIS DAY OUR DAILY BREAD, AND FORGIVE OUR TRESPASSES AS WE FORGIVE THOSE WHO TRESPASS AGAINST US

These two petitions are closely related. We are, in effect, asking for two kinds of sustenance: sustenance for ourselves personally and sustenance for ourselves as members of the human family.

**Personal sustenance.** Immediately we are faced with a question. Is the Lord's Prayer literally asking for physical bread for the body? Yes, as most of the human race goes to bed hungry every night.

Those in affluent societies may think of this prayer for bread as either out of touch with reality or as merely symbolic. It is very real. There is hunger, even famine, among millions of starving people throughout the world. We are therefore begging God to open the hearts of those who are rich in material possessions to share with those who are lacking even the necessities of life.

**Spiritual nourishment.** Still on the personal plane, we have need of more than just bread for the body. St. Pius X, who restored early and frequent Holy Communion in the Church, declared that the primary bread we ask for in the *Our Father* is daily sustenance through the Holy Eucharist. In the early Church, the faithful assisted at Mass and received Communion every day. They needed it to keep them faithful to Christ in what we call the Ages of Persecution. But we are now living in the Age of Martyrs. More men, women, and children have shed their blood for Christ since 1900 than in all the previous nineteen centuries put together. We, more than anyone in Christian history, need the daily reception of the Body of Christ to keep us supernaturally alive in the grace of God.

**Preservation and progress of human society.** We do not usually associate forgiving love with benefitting human society. But we should.

In this fifth petition we are certainly praying for God's mercy. We are asking him to be merciful to us as we are merciful to those who sin against us. We are begging him for the charity to forgive so that he might exercise his divine charity in forgiving us.

But that is not all. We are also asking God to give us a share in his own understanding love in using sinners for the advancement of his kingdom. This does not mean ignoring the weakness or sinfulness of people. It does mean that we rely on God's wisdom and the power that only he can give. He will enable us to see the good in others and draw on this goodness for the progress, and not just the preservation, of human society on earth as a prelude to that heavenly society for which we were made.

## Maxim of St. Augustine

"There are many kinds of alms the giving of which helps us to obtain pardon for our sins. But none is greater than that by which we forgive from our heart a sin that someone has committed against us."

| 48 | LEAD US NOT INTO TEMPTATION, BUT DELIVER US FROM EVIL |

The closing petitions of the Our Father touch each of us individually. We are all subject to temptation and we all need to be delivered from evil.

**Benefitting from temptations.** The word "temptation" is ambiguous. Literally it means to be tested or tried. In this sense, even Christ was tempted, not that he might be tested for fidelity to his Father, but that he might endure the humiliation of being tried by the devil who, as we saw, was not sure that Jesus was the incarnate God.

Unlike Christ, our temptations are so many tests by which we prove our loyalty to God. Unlike Christ, we are tempted not only from the outside, the world, and the devil. We are also tempted from the inside, by the sinful drives of concupiscence which is the result of original sin.

In God's providence, our temptations are not to lead us into sin but to strengthen our commitment to Christ.

What, then, are we asking when we pray not to be led into temptation? We are asking for prudence and fortitude:

- Prudence in order to avoid exposing ourselves recklessly or needlessly into temptation; prudence to foresee the occasions of sin; prudence to anticipate how to cope with unavoidable temptations; and prudence to be armed with supernatural wisdom to draw closer to God because of the temptations.

- Fortitude in order to forego the satisfaction which a temptation promises to give and endure the suffering which a temptation claims we shall be spared; fortitude to persevere in a good work in spite of the temptation to give up; and fortitude to accept the opportunity of assimilation to Christ who allowed himself to be tempted by the devil.

**Deliverance from evil.** We know what evil is in general. It is anything contrary to the will. If it is contrary to the divine will, we call it moral evil or sin. If it is contrary to the created will, we call it physical evil or pain.

In the closing petition of the Lord's Prayer we are asking to be delivered from both forms of evil but in different ways:

- We ask to be delivered from sin absolutely. We entreat Our Lord to protect us from ever again committing a mortal sin. But we also beg him to help us overcome venial sins. In a word, we are praying to become more and more sinless as we approach the threshold of eternity.
- We ask to be delivered from pain conditionally. The condition is that the pain would not draw us closer to God or might, in fact, be spiritually harmful.

Pain can be spiritually profitable. To that extent we should embrace it as a means of purifying our souls and making us more pleasing in the eyes of God.

One evil we ask God to deliver us from without reserve is the evil of eternal damnation or hell.

## Maxims of the Saints

"The more desperate things seem, the more we must hope in God. Where human efforts fail, there before us waits the divine assistance." **St. Ignatius**

"It is characteristic of the divine goodness to protect with greater wisdom whatever the devil assaults with greater violence." St. Ignatius

"All hope consists in Confession. Believe it firmly. Do not doubt, do not hesitate, never despair of the mercy of God. Hope and have confidence in Confession." St. Isidore of Seville

"The way to overcome the devil when he excites feelings of hatred for those who injure us is immediately to pray for their conversion." St. John Vianney

"I do not trust myself as long as I am in this body of death... The hostile flesh always draws me toward death, that is, toward enticements unlawful to indulge in." St. Patrick

"We cannot command our final perseverance, but must ask it from God." St. Thomas Aquinas

"To know whom to avoid is a great means of saving our souls."
St. Thomas Aquinas

"Occupy your minds with good thoughts, or the enemy will fill them with bad ones. Unoccupied, they cannot be." St. Thomas More

"He who remembers the presence of God is less open to other thoughts, especially bad thoughts... In two ways the presence of God is an antidote against sin. First because God sees us, and secondly, because we see God." St. Ignatius

# 17

# The Public Ministry of Jesus

FOLLOWING THE SERMON ON THE MOUNT, St. Ignatius offers a series of meditations on the public ministry of Christ. Certain features in this ministry stand out in the Spiritual Exercises:

- Christ gave the apostles the opportunity to preach while they were still in training.
- Christ forgave notorious sinners.
- Christ worked astounding miracles and gave the apostles a share in his own miraculous powers.
- The enemies of Christ were marshalling their forces to destroy him.

## 49 | CHRIST CALMS THE STORM

The focus of the Sermon on the Mount was the elevated moral teaching of the Savior. What he demanded of his followers was such self-sacrifice as no one in the Old Testament had ever taught before.

Following the miracle at Cana, Ignatius chooses another physical miracle to strengthen our faith in Christ's authority to lay superhuman demands on those who believe in his name.

**Christ is asleep.** Every detail in the life of Christ is important. A great crowd had assembled. But Jesus was tired. "He gave orders to go across the sea" (Mt 8:23). Once in the boat, a great storm arose, "... so that the boat was covered by the waves; but he was asleep" (Mt 8:24b).

Christ was human. He could become exhausted and in need of rest. On this occasion he was so tired that even the storm did not wake him up.

The lesson for us is never to doubt God's awareness of our trials. He is never asleep although he wants to test our faith in his care by allowing us to wonder.

**The miracle after the doubt.** Aroused by the storm, the disciples woke Jesus and cried out, "... Lord, save us! We are perishing!" (Mt 8:25b). His answer was to be expected. "... Why are you fearful, O you of little faith?..." (Mt 8:26b). There is much more to Christ's rebuke than we might suppose. Naturally speaking the disciples had reason to fear. But Christ was there with them. If they really believed who he was, why be afraid? Applied to ourselves, if we really believe that God is behind every "happening" in our lives, why should we be afraid?

Then to confirm their faith in his almighty power, Christ "... rebuked the wind and the sea, and there came a great calm" (Mt 8:26b). The reaction of the disciples was spontaneous. They asked themselves, "... What manner of man is this that even the wind and the sea obey him?" (Mt 8:27b).

Another lesson. The more frightening a situation, the more God is ready to work a miracle to calm the storms in our life—on one condition, that we trust in his power and love. Our confidence is part of his providence.

### Maxims of the Saints

"The weight of fear is the anchor of the heart." Pope St. Gregory I

"It will be enough to receive the evils which come upon us from time to time, without anticipating them by the imagination."

St. Francis de Sales

## 50 | CHRIST WALKS UPON THE WATERS

Six chapters after the previous event, St. Matthew describes another miraculous experience. Christ had just fed the multitude by the marvelous multiplication of the loaves and fishes. Then he dismissed the crowd after telling his disciples to get into the boat. He went up the nearby mountain by himself to pray.

**Christ comes to the disciples at sea.** After hours of prayer alone, Jesus comes walking on the water toward his disciples. Meanwhile a storm breaks out over the waters. When the disciples saw Jesus they were terrified. " '… It is a ghost,' they cried out. But Jesus reassured them, 'Take courage; it is I, do not be afraid' " (Mt 14:26b-27).

**Peter comes to Christ.** No sooner had Christ said it was he, than Peter spoke to Jesus. "Lord, if it is you, bid me come to you over the water." To which Jesus replied, "Come."

Peter got out of the boat and began walking on the water toward Jesus. But as he felt the strong wind, he was afraid. Immediately he began to sink, and called out, "Lord, save me!" Jesus, still standing on the water, stretched out his hand and took hold of Peter. Again, as with the storm at sea, Jesus rebuked Peter, "O, you of little faith, why did you doubt?" With that the wind died down. After everyone was in the boat, the disciples prostrated themselves before Jesus, "Truly you are the Son of God" (Mt 14:28-33).

**The need of courage in the apostolate.** St. Ignatius consciously placed this meditation just before sending the apostles out to preach. They would need all the encouragement they could get from the Master before they started their apostolic ministry.

Following Christ in proclaiming his word to an unsympathetic world is literally walking on water. There is no headway. There are only sinking feet—unless Christ works the continuing miracle of making his teaching acceptable to a self-preoccupied world.

## Maxims of the Saints

"The principal act of courage is to endure and withstand dangers firmly, rather than to attack them." **St. Thomas Aquinas**

"There is only one thing to be feared... only one trial and that is sin. I have told you this over and over again. All the rest is beside the point; whether you talk of plots, feuds, betrayals, slanders, abuses, confiscations of property, exile, swords, open sea, or universal war. Whatever they may be, they are all fugitive and perishable. They touch the mortal body but wreak no harm on the watchful soul." **St. John Chrysostom**

## 51     CHRIST SENDS THE APOSTLES TO PREACH

One of the most detailed instructions that Christ ever gave was to the apostles as he sent them to preach the Gospel while he was still with them visibly in Palestine. This was long before his final commission just before his Ascension.

**Power over demons and sickness.** Not surprisingly, Jesus first gave the apostles power over the evil spirit. As Ignatius never tires pointing out, those who proclaim the gospel are in deadly competition with the devil. Power over the evil one is the essence of the apostolate.

So too the power of healing sickness. The apostles were enabled to work miracles of healing as a manifestation of God's approval of their proclaiming the Word of God.

**Prudence and patience.** They were being sent, Christ tells them, "like sheep in the midst of wolves." Consequently, they should be "wise as serpents and simple as doves." These two injunctions, St. Ignatius interprets as prudence and patience.

- Why prudence? Because the apostle must be always on guard not to be seduced by the sinners he has come to convert. Moreover, they can be more cunning in seducing him than he in converting them.

- Why patience? Because zeal in the apostolate always arouses opposition. Sheep and doves are the figures of speech that Christ uses to express the readiness to suffer for proclaiming Christ. Only the special grace of God will enable us to combine the shrewdness and simplicity that winning souls to Christ demands.

## Maxims of St. Ignatius

"In treating with men, we must speak little and listen much. Even these few words we should speak as if the whole world were to hear them, though we are talking only to one person."

"Innocence and holiness of life are of themselves more powerful and far preferable to all other gifts. But without prudence and the art of dealing with the world, they remain incomplete and incapable of guiding others."

# 18

# Preludes to the Passion of Christ

St. Ignatius provides for a series of meditations toward the close of Christ's public ministry. The three that we shall choose are: the Transfiguration, the Raising of Lazarus, and Palm Sunday.

Each of these has a library of commentary among the masters of the spiritual life, and each is a logical bridge between the life and preaching of the Savior and his passion and death, which are the focus of the third week of the Spiritual Exercises.

## 52 | THE TRANSFIGURATION

"The principal purpose of the transfiguration," according to Pope Leo the Great, "was to remove from the hearts of the disciples the scandal of the cross." Just preceding the transfiguration, Christ had foretold his passion and declared "… If anyone wishes to come after me, let him deny himself, and take up his cross and follow me" (Mt 16:24b).

**The miraculous event.** St. Matthew records that, "… Jesus took Peter, James, and his brother, John, and led them up a high mountain by themselves, and was transfigured before them. And his face shone as the sun, and his garments became white as snow" (Mt 17:1b-2).

The three disciples whom Christ selectively chose to witness the transfiguration were the same three whom he would selectively take into the Garden of Gethsemane for his agony. In the mind of Christ, these two events go together. The transfiguration was to prepare the disciples for the Savior's passion.

**Jesus speaks with Moses and Elijah.** Why, we may ask, would these ancient heroes appear in conversation with Jesus? Because they represent the highest reaches of the Old Testament: Moses the great lawgiver and Elijah the leading prophet. Jesus came to fulfill both the law and the prophets of the Old Covenant. He was their fulfillment.

Yet Christ spoke with them to teach us that the Old Testament is all about him; that we are to see in him the pattern for our moral life and the source of all we believe.

**The voice from heaven.** Then the disciples heard a voice from heaven, saying, "… This is my beloved Son, in whom I am well pleased; hear him" (Mt 17:5b).

Even as happened at his baptism, the voice of the heavenly Father attests to Christ's divinity, to the Father being pleased with his Son's humanity, and also to the duty we have to listen to what Jesus teaches us in audible words as the Son of Man speaking with the authority of the Son of God.

Jesus strictly forbade the three witnesses to tell anyone about the transfiguration, "… until the Son of Man has risen from the dead" (Mt 17:9b, JB). Why the prohibition? Because so many of his contemporaries had a false idea about the Messiah as an earthly king; and because the vision might be misunderstood as a hallucination which would detract from the credibility of those who had witnessed the transfiguration.

## Maxim of St. Thomas Aquinas

"In order to strengthen the hearts of his disciples… [Jesus] sets before them those who had exposed themselves to death for God's sake: since Moses braved death in opposing Pharaoh, and Elijah in opposing Ahab."

## 53 THE RAISING OF LAZARUS

The single longest sustained miracle narrative in the Gospels is St. John's account of the raising of Lazarus from the grave.

Actually the whole of chapter eleven of the fourth Gospel is a prelude to the miracle, the miracle itself, and the effect this had on the enemies of Christ.

**Sickness and death of Lazarus.** Mary and Martha, the sisters of Lazarus, sent word to Jesus that their brother was seriously sick. But Jesus delayed two days before going to see Lazarus. Meanwhile he told his disciples that "... Lazarus sleeps. But I am going that I may wake him from sleep" (Jn 11:11b). Because the disciples misunderstood him, he explained that "Lazarus is dead," adding "I rejoice on your account that I was not there that you may believe..." (Jn 11:15a).

More than once, Christ spoke of persons who had died as being asleep. This has profound implications. What Christ was saying is that, as Master of life and death, persons who have died are, for him, people who are merely asleep. He has the power to "wake them" from the sleep of death.

**Christ the resurrection and the life.** Having arrived at the tomb, Jesus declared, "... I am the resurrection and the life. He who believes in me, even if he die, shall live, and whoever lives and believes in me shall never die" (Jn 11:25b-26).

Christ is here speaking of two kinds of life and two kinds of resurrection. He is Master of both.

- Christ is Master of our bodily life and resurrection. Except for him, who is God, we would not have the bodily human life we possess. As God he also has the power to raise dead bodies back to life.
- Christ is Master of our spiritual life and resurrection. Except for him, who is the God-man, we would not have the supernatural life of the soul, which he won for us by his

own passion and death. He therefore also has the power to restore "dead" souls back to the life of grace.

**Christ raises Lazarus from the grave.** Seeing the people weeping at the grave, Jesus also wept. He then ordered the stone to be removed from the entrance to the tomb and prayed to his Father. Part of his prayer was to say that he was praying so that the people standing around "… may believe that you sent me. Then in a loud voice, he cried out, 'Lazarus, come forth!' And Lazarus came out of the tomb, alive" (Jn 11:42b-44a).

As a result, many of the witnesses of this miracle believed in Jesus. But some went away unbelieving to report to the Pharisees who promptly decided this was too much. "If we let him alone as he is, all will believe in him, and the Romans will come and take away both our place and our nation" (Jn 11:48).

Christ's passion followed as a logical consequence. The stubborn pride of his enemies prevented them from believing in him even when he openly raised a decaying corpse from the grave.

## Maxims of the Saints

"Faith opens the door to understanding; unbelief closes it."

St. Augustine

"What is more against reason than by reason to attempt to transcend reason? And what is more against faith than to be unwilling to believe what reason cannot attain?"   St. Bernard

## 54 | PALM SUNDAY

On Palm Sunday, the church commemorates Christ's triumphal entry into Jerusalem when olive and palm branches were strewn in his path. It is also the opening of Holy Week.

St. Ignatius makes it the last meditation before reflecting on the degrees of humility and deciding on the election or chosen decision of the Spiritual Exercises.

**Christ's directives to the disciples.** Anticipating his passion, Christ instructed two of his disciples to bring a beast of burden and its colt to Jerusalem. They did so and laid their garments on the animals for Jesus to ride one of them.

**The triumphal entry.** As Jesus rode into Jerusalem, most of the crowd laid their cloaks on the road while others were cutting branches from olive and palm trees. These were then carried in their hands as symbols of triumph. The crowds were Galilean pilgrims who came out of Jerusalem to see him. Some walked in front of Jesus, and others behind him. They kept crying out, "… Hosanna to the Son of David! Blessed is he who comes in the name of the Lord! Hosanna in the highest!" (Mt 21:9b).

When he entered Jerusalem, however, the whole city was thrown into commotion. But the jubilant crowds kept on saying, "This is Jesus the prophet from Nazareth of Galilee."

**The implications.** It is not necessary to assume that the same crowds that called out "Hosanna to the Son of David!" on Palm Sunday were the same ones who cried out, "Crucify Him! Crucify Him!" on Good Friday.

What is certain is that Christ had strong admirers and strong opponents among the people of his native Palestine. Already on Palm Sunday, some of the Pharisees told him to rebuke his followers for their display of fervor. Jesus answered that if the people were to be silent, the very stones would cry out.

It was on this occasion that Jesus wept over Jerusalem. He foretold how the city would be besieged and destroyed, "… because you have not known the time of your visitation" (Lk 19:44b).

A generation later Jerusalem was to be stormed by the Roman armies. Every word of Christ's dire prediction was fulfilled to the letter. God is merciful; that is why he became human, to save a sinful world. But God is also just. Sinners are punished here on earth and, if they do not repent, in the life to come.

## Maxims of the Saints

"Sin is a fearful evil, but easy to cure for him who by repentance puts it away from him." St. Cyril of Jerusalem

"Evil clings to our nature like rust to iron, or dirt to the body. But as rust is not produced by the iron worker, nor dirt by the parent, so also evil is not produced by God. He gave man conscience and reason to avoid all evil, knowing that it is harmful and prepares torment for him. So pay strict attention and when you meet some man possessed by power and wealth, be in no way beguiled by the demon to pander to him. But let death immediately stand before your eyes; and you will never desire anything bad or worldly." St. Anthony the Great

# 19

## Degrees of Humility and the Retreat Election

THE PURPOSE OF THE SPIRITUAL EXERCISES is to bring the retreatant to consider the concerns of this day, that is, making definite choices in one's life according to the will of God.

In a sense, this has been the underlying theme of all the meditations so far. But here the retreatant is to draw on all the preceding insights, building on them and relying on the help of divine grace to reach a conclusion and then determine to pursue certain resolutions.

Our plan for the day is to cover three crucial areas of meditation, namely, the Three Degrees of Humility, Choosing a Way of Life, and Amending One's Way of Life.

## 55 | THE THREE DEGREES OF HUMILITY

In this meditation retreatants should ask themselves what level of humility they have the grace to practice? The reason for this basic question is to reach a balanced decision on God's will for oneself.

St. Ignatius distinguishes three levels or degrees of generosity towards God. Each level is called a degree of humility because it means the degree of my responsiveness to the grace of God.

**First degree of humility.** We have a free will in order to voluntarily cooperate with the will of God.

On the most fundamental level, he wants us to do certain things as a condition for reaching our heavenly destiny. The divine will is manifested in certain commandments that are binding under penalty of mortal sin. A comprehensive list of such sins was given by St. Paul in the first chapter of his letter to the Romans. After enumerating these sins, the apostle says, "Life eternal he will give to those who by patience in good works seek glory and honor and immortality; but wrath and indignation to those who are contentious and who do not submit to the truth but assent to iniquity" (Rom 2:7-8).

I have the first kind of humility if I would not offend God mortally even if this meant the sacrifice of everything, including my life.

**Second degree of humility.** In this degree I am internally detached from all creatures, for example, riches or poverty, honor or dishonor, provided in either alternative I would give equal service to God and assure the salvation of my soul. Moreover, I would not, under any circumstances, want to commit even a venial sin.

**Third degree of humility.** This degree presupposes the first two, but goes beyond them. How so? I positively prefer poverty with Christ's poor rather than riches. So, too, I prefer insults with Christ who was loaded with them; and I want to be "accounted as worthless and a fool for Christ rather than to be esteemed as wise and prudent in this world. My motive is my love for Christ. I personally prefer what he chose out of love for me."

The only condition is that God would be equally served and glorified. But as far as I am concerned, this is my attitude. Love seeks assimilation to the one who is loved.

## Maxims of the Saints

"He who renounces all his possessions for Christ's sake, exposes himself to no danger, neither spiritual nor corporal. For spiritual danger ensues from poverty when the latter is not voluntary;

because those who are unwillingly poor, through the desire of money-getting, fall into many sins according to 2 Timothy 6:9. 'They that will become rich, fall into temptation and into the snare of the devil.' This attachment is put away by those who embrace voluntary poverty, but it gathers strength in those who have wealth." **St. Thomas Aquinas**

"Consider within you how Jesus Christ was crucified, naked, blasphemed, calumniated, forsaken, overwhelmed with every kind of injury, sadness and toil; and reflect that your sufferings can in no way be likened to his, either in kind or degree, and that you can never bear anything for him compared to what he has borne for you." **St. Francis de Sales**

## 56     CHOOSING A WAY OF LIFE

St. Ignatius devotes several pages in the Spiritual Exercises to choosing a way of life. This is not surprising since his own experience of choosing a way of life is what originally produced the Exercises.

As a prelude to this meditation, it should be seen as suitable for everyone including those who have already made a lifetime decision. They can deepen their commitment and purify their motives. They can also see what is so necessary that our primary purpose in any state of life should be the service of God. The actual way of life thus becomes a means to achieving the primary goal.

**Matters for making a choice.** It is assumed that the object of my choice is something morally good and pleasing to God.

The actual choice may be an unchangeable one, like marriage, the priesthood, or the religious life. Or it may be regarding something that is changeable, for example, a profession, or employment, or enterprise, or location.

Suppose an unchangeable choice had been made, "for instance

by marriage or the priesthood... since it cannot be undone, no further choice is possible." However, says Ignatius, the following should be noted:

> If the choice has not been made as it should have been, and with due order, that is, if it was not made without inordinate attachments, one should be sorry for this, and take care to live well in the life he has chosen.

The author of the Exercises assumes that commitments to marriage or the priesthood are unchangeable. It is impossible to exaggerate the importance of this presupposition, given the widespread instability in what should be permanent states of life.

**Times for making a good choice.** There are traditionally three times when a wise choice of a way of life can be made. They may be identified with three words: miracle, discernment, and tranquility.

- Miraculous, direct invitation, as found in the call of the apostles and seen in the lives of some of the saints.
- Discerning the Spirit through strong experience of desolation and consolation.

Both of the above are extraordinary. That is why St. Ignatius devotes so much attention to the "third time," which is tranquility of soul. He proposes two methods for making a choice of a state—or way—of life during a period "when the soul is not agitated by different spirits, and has free and peaceful use of its natural powers."

**The first method.** The first method is basically a prayerful weighing of the pros and cons, and asking God to enlighten my mind on his will for me. Of critical importance is my sincere desire to do what "is more for the glory of God and the salvation of my soul."

**The second method.** The second method is a set of rules to be applied. They are actually four questions that I should ask myself:

- Is my attraction for a particular way of life or course of action dictated solely by my love for God?

- What advice would I give to someone whose spiritual welfare I wished to promote? Would I give myself the same counsel?
- What would I wish to have chosen if I were at the moment of death? Make the same choice now.
- If I were standing before Christ my judge on the last day, what choice would I make? Again, make the same choice now.

## Maxims of St. Francis de Sales

"A good vocation is simply a firm and constant will in which the called person has to serve God in the way and in the places to which almighty God has called him."

"If a person shows a firm and persevering determination to serve God in the manner and place to which his divine majesty calls him, he gives the best proof we can have that he has a true vocation."

## 57 | AMENDING ONE'S WAY OF LIFE

This meditation is the capstone to the Spiritual Exercises because of its sound practicality. All the meditations which follow are meant to strengthen our retreat resolutions. But this meditation deals explicitly with the one resolution that affects most persons who make a retreat. In answer to a single question: "How do I go about reforming my life?" They are told to do three things:

- examine the purpose of your life;
- examine the means by which you can fulfill this purpose; and
- surrender your self-love, your self-will, and your self-interests.

**What is the purpose of my life?** This is the bedrock of any rational decision in life and certainly a decision about reforming one's moral behavior. Unless I first ask myself, "Why am I in this world?"—it is logically impossible to even talk about amendment or reformation. But if my life here on earth is the divinely ordained means of reaching an eternal destiny, then, but only then, does it make sense to ask whether there is something out of order that needs to be changed.

So true is this, that most people's "problems," as they call them, are due to the fact that they do not evaluate everything in their lives from the vantage point of eternity.

**Necessary means for amendment.** Somewhat surprisingly, St. Ignatius concentrates on the disposition of one's material resources. He knew, of course, that there are many possible ways of amending or reforming one's life. Yet he also knew that for most people, their lifestyle, to use modern jargon, is basic to any serious moral improvement. It was not coincidental that Our Lord placed poverty of spirit at the head of the Beatitudes.

This was also crystalized in Christ's declaration that, "... You cannot serve God and mammon" (Mt 6:24b), where mammon stands for worldly goods. So true is this that a fair estimate of how serious we are about living a good moral life is to ask ourselves how detached are we from the passing goods of this world.

**Self-surrender.** The third step in amending one's life is to resolve to practice self-surrender.

In the last analysis this is what amendment is all about. Our natural bent is to self-satisfaction, self-advantage, self-seeking, and self-love. What is the remedy? It is to "desire and seek nothing except the greater praise and glory of God our Lord as the aim of all" that we do. In other words, our progress in the spiritual life will be in proportion to our sacrifice of self, offered to God on the altar of our daily lives.

### Maxims of St. Ignatius

"We should make more account of renouncing self-will than of raising others from the dead."

"Each person should convince himself that he will make progress in the spiritual life in proportion to his detachment from self and the desire of self advantage."

"The empty honors of earth cannot satisfy you. Your heart is not narrow enough for the whole world to suffice for it; nothing but God can fill it. I am not trying to extinguish your ardor for glory, nor inspire you with mean thoughts. Be ambitious, be high-minded, but let your ambition aim higher by despising all that is perishable."

# THIRD WEEK

# Introduction to the Third Week

THE PURPOSE OF THE THIRD WEEK is to consolidate our resolutions for the retreat and to further motivate ourselves to give ourselves entirely to the following of Christ.

During the meditations for this week, our focus will be on the passion of Christ, from the Last Supper to Calvary and the burial. Although the length of time covered by the passion is less than twenty-four hours, the Holy Spirit inspired the evangelists to devote the most extensive care to preserving every significant feature of this historic day.

St. Ignatius gives the director considerable leeway in the number of meditations for the third week. He provides for up to seven days. Our plan is to devote six full days' meditation as follows:

- The Last Supper, the Holy Eucharist, and Priesthood.
- The Agony in the Garden, Betrayal, and Taking Christ Captive.
- Christ before Annas, Caiaphas, and the Sanhedrin.
- Christ before Pilate and Herod, Condemnation to Death.
- The Way of the Cross.
- The Crucifixion, Seven Last Words, and Burial.

With such an ocean of detail on the passion in the Gospels, it is recommended that the retreatant read the New Testament account of what took place on Holy Thursday and Good Friday.

It is also advisable during the third week to keep oneself more or less consciously in the presence of Our Lord in the Blessed Sacrament. He instituted the Eucharist on the night before he died and consummated this abiding gift of his love on Calvary.

# 20

# The Last Supper

### I. Washing the Feet, Judas, and the New Commandment

THERE ARE FIVE ACCOUNTS of the Last Supper. St. Matthew narrates the institution of the Holy Eucharist and Christ's prediction of Peter's triple denial of his Master. St. Mark does the same. St. Luke adds the episode about the contention among the apostles as to which of them was the greatest. St. John does not record the institution of the Eucharist, but devotes no less than five chapters to the Last Supper (13 through 17), including:

- Christ washing the feet of the apostles;
- Judas identified as betrayer;
- Christ's assurance to his followers;
- the new commandment of love;
- the world's hatred of Christ;
- the role of the Holy Spirit; and
- Christ's prayer for unity.

Besides the synoptic Gospels, St. Paul narrates the institution of the Eucharist with additional explanations on the Real Presence and the Sacrifice of the Mass. We shall reserve the Holy Eucharist for tomorrow's meditations.

## 58 | WASHING THE FEET OF THE APOSTLES

Only the fourth evangelist describes the mysterious action of Christ washing the feet of his apostles. Also, only St. John gives us the long discourse of the Savior at the Last Supper, including his revelation of the new commandment of selfless charity.

**Christ assumes the role of servant.** Washing the feet of a guest was a custom of hospitality in the East. But it was always done by a servant. This time Jesus himself put off his outer garments, put on an apron, poured water into a basin, and began washing the feet of his disciples.

This was the introduction to both the dialogue that was to follow and the basic lesson of selfless servant love that Jesus was to teach his followers.

**Dialogue with Peter.** When Jesus came to wash Peter's feet, Peter protested. Jesus warned him, "... If I do not wash your feet, you shall have no part with me" (Jn 13:8b). Peter relented and told the Savior to wash not only his feet but his hands and feet as well.

Jesus went on to explain why he was washing the disciples' feet. It was to cleanse them, but he added, "... You are not all clean" (Jn 13:11b). He was referring to Judas. Even washing Judas' feet would not cleanse an unrepentant sinner.

**Following Christ's example of service.** After he had washed their feet, Jesus draws the fundamental lesson he wanted them to learn. Like him, they were to be of service to others especially in reconciling others with God.

There is a twofold lesson here that is meant for everyone:

- We are true disciples of Christ if we imitate his example of ministering to the needs of other people.
- The deepest need that most people have is to draw closer to God by being cleansed of their disordered self-love, which is the root of all sin.

**Maxims of the Saints**

"To sin is human, but to persist in sin is devilish."

**St. Catherine of Siena**

"What a task it is to purge a soul here below and restore her with no further purgatory to her pristine purity... She must pass through many cruel sufferings that she may gain merit by many and grievous penances." **St. Catherine of Genoa**

---

## 59 | JUDAS THE BETRAYER

All four evangelists describe at length how Jesus was betrayed by Judas Iscariot. Among these, St. John's description is the most extensive.

**The prediction.** During the Last Supper, Jesus says solemnly, "... Amen, amen, I say to you, one of you will betray me" (Jn 13:21b).

Immediately the disciples began to look at one another, wondering whom Jesus could mean. Peter turned to John, who was seated next to Jesus, and asked him "Who is it of whom he speaks?" John, in turn asked Jesus, "... Lord, who is it?" (Jn 13:25b).

Jesus answered, "... It is he for whom I shall dip the bread and give it to him..." (Jn 13:26b). The moment Judas received the morsel, Satan entered into him. He then left the upper room quickly to carry out his crime. The evangelist adds, "... It was night" (Jn 13:30b).

**The motive.** Volumes of explanations have been given by masters of the spiritual life about Judas' act of betrayal. Among the motives offered, two especially stand out, a weak faith and the love of money.

We know that the apostles were not too strong in their faith in Christ's divinity and his redemptive mission. But we are shocked at Judas' complaint over the pound of ointment that Lazarus'

sister Mary poured over the feet of Jesus. "Why was this ointment not sold for three hundred denarii and given to the poor?"
(Jn 12:5). The evangelist explains why Judas said this. "... He
was a thief, and holding the purse, used to take what was put in
it" (Jn 12:6b).

**Spiritual implications.** The name of Judas has entered the
vocabulary of all nations. It stands for betrayal by those in high
office who have been trusted by others and entrusted with great
spiritual responsibilities.

Historians of the church have not hesitated to draw some
sobering conclusions. In the mysterious providence of God,
Judas is a lesson for all of us. We are prepared against every possible shock to our consciences. If Judas could be described as
Our Lord's apostle, why should some notorious ecclesiastic not
be a successor of the apostles?

### Maxims of the Saints

"A cleric who engages in business and who rises from poverty to
wealth and from obscurity to a high position, avoid as you would
the plague." St. Jerome

"It is indeed a monstrous combination to have the highest dignity joined with a soul that is base, the highest place with the
lowest conduct, exalted speech with an idle hand, much talk and
no fruit, a solemn exterior with frivolous actions, a tremendous
authority with little strength." St. Bernard

## 60  THE NEW COMMANDMENT

No sooner had Judas left the room on his errand of treachery
than Jesus told the rest of the disciples that he was elevating
human morality beyond anything conceivable before the
Incarnation. "A new commandment I give you that you love

one another; that as I have loved you, you also love one another. By this will all men know that you are my disciples if you have love for one another" (Jn 13:35-35).

We therefore ask: What precisely is new about the new commandment of Christ; and how is the observance of this law of love a proof that someone is a disciple of Christ?

**What is new about Christ's commandment?** In order to understand this question, we must return to Christ's Sermon on the Mount. He insisted that he had not come to abolish the law or the prophets but to fulfill them. In no other aspect of human behavior is this more clear than in the duty we have to love others.

In the Old Testament, the chosen people were commanded, "... You shall love your neighbor as yourself..." (Lv 19:18b).

This was a high ethic, which Christ himself reconfirmed. It was a precept binding on every Israelite as an individual. It also made each person's love of self the norm for loving someone else.

What did Christ do? He extended the commandment of love to all his followers as a mutual imperative. "... Love one another..." he ordered (Jn 13:34b). But more still, he made his own love of us the norm for our selfless love of one another.

Words cannot describe the sublimity of altruism which this implies.

- It is the generosity of God who became man out of love for us.
- It is the mercy of God who became man that he might suffer and die out of love for us who by our sins rejected his love.
- It is the selflessness of God who gained nothing for himself by his redemption and too often has received only indifference and ingratitude in return for his ineffable love.

**Proof of being disciples of Christ.** It is a verdict of history that selfless charity has been the hallmark of authentic Christianity.

It was this single virtue that historians tell us mainly converted the pagan world of the Roman Empire to the Catholic faith. Christ-like charity, we may say, is the final mark of the Church's credibility. Why should this be true? Because human nature, left to itself, is profoundly selfish. It requires nothing less than the almighty power of God, become man, to enable human beings to love one another with a selfless charity inspired by infinite love become incarnate.

## Maxims of the Saints

"Let us love one another and thus prove that we are disciples of the Truth. And in this mutual charity let us be careful of three things, for God is charity and we should be anxious about nothing but charity: that it may come to birth, that it may grow, and that it may be preserved." St. Bernard

"We should strive to cultivate in ourselves seven sentiments or dispositions toward our neighbor. The first is, by a compassionate generosity, to sympathize with him in his afflictions and misfortunes, as if they were our own. The second is to rejoice in his prosperity as our own. The third is to calmly bear with his defects, to suffer patiently whatever is disagreeable in him, and to pardon readily the offenses which he may have committed against us. The fourth is to act with sweetness and affability toward all men, to wish them well... The fifth is to prefer others to our selves, to have a humble and sincere regard for our brethren... The sixth is to live in peace and concord with everyone, as far as we are able, and according to God... The seventh is to be ready to lay down our life for the salvation of the brethren." St. Vincent Ferrer

# 21

# The Last Supper

## II. The Holy Eucharist and the Priesthood

IN THE SPIRITUAL EXERCISES, Christ's institution of the Holy Eucharist and the priesthood is only a part of the meditation on the Last Supper. But the marvelous development of doctrine that has taken place since St. Ignatius warrant our devoting a whole day to this bilateral mystery.

It is bilateral because the Eucharist and the priesthood belong together by divine association. Christ is the eternal high priest who continues dispensing his grace of salvation on a sinful world. The principal channel of these graces is the Holy Eucharist as a sacrament three times over:

- the sacrifice-sacrament of the Mass;
- the communion-sacrament of Holy Communion; and
- the presence-sacrament of his abiding Real Presence outside of Mass and Communion.

But there would be no Eucharist without the priesthood which the Church infallibly teaches was instituted at the Last Supper.

Our focus in the present meditation is on the Holy Eucharist. Before reflecting on this mystery of truth, however, we should at least briefly ask Our Lord to help us appreciate the great gift he gave us when on Holy Thursday night he consecrated his apostles the first bishops of his Church. He then gave them the power to do what he had done, to change bread and wine into his own living Body and Blood and to transmit this power to others until the end of time.

This transmission of Eucharistic power from Christ to his apostles is especially clear in the narrative of the Last Supper in the Gospel of St. Luke and the First Letter of St. Paul to the Corinthians.

Under divine inspiration, Paul and his disciple Luke record those memorable words of Jesus when he told the apostles, not once but twice, to "do this"—change bread and wine into his Body and Blood—"... in remembrance of me" (Lk 22:19-20; 1 Cor 11:24b).

The separate consecration of the bread and wine into the Body and Blood of Christ signifies the separation of Christ's Body and Blood on Calvary. If Christ could die, he would, every time Mass is offered. His readiness to die is his act of oblation now in an unbloody manner; but it is no less real a sacrifice than his bloody death on the cross.

## 61 | INSTITUTION OF THE SACRIFICE OF THE MASS

As Catholics we believe that Christ's death on the cross merited the salvation of the world. His precious blood shed on the cross won for the whole human race all the graces needed for salvation until the end of time.

But we also believe that, the moment Christ died, the Church he founded came into existence. And it is through this Church that the graces of Calvary are communicated to humanity, especially through the sacrament of the Eucharist.

**Graces of mercy and expiation.** The sacrifice of the Mass, just because it is offered, obtains mercy from God for the remission of the guilt and punishment due to sin. Moreover, these blessings are available through the Mass not only for ourselves but for others, both living still on earth and for the souls in purgatory.

**Graces of self-surrender.** We do not always think of the Mass as a sacrament. But we should. Every time that Mass is offered, Christ the eternal priest pours out his sacramental graces on the whole of humanity.

What kind of graces does he give through the Mass? The graces we need to live sacrificial lives. In practice this means the light and strength we need to surrender our wills to the loving but demanding will of God.

**Our cooperation.** The graces of the Mass are available. But we must do our part. Three recommendations that go back to apostolic times:

- We should attend Mass as often as we can.
- We should participate in the Mass as actively as we can, especially by our daily lives of sacrifice.
- We should have Masses offered for our own intentions and for others, as the single most powerful source of supernatural blessings available to the human family.

### Maxims of the Saints

"Holy Mass is an achievement of God wherein he places before our view all the love he has borne us; in a sense it is the synthesis, the sum of all his benefits bestowed upon us." **St. Bonaventure**

"O eternal Father, permit me to offer you the Heart of Jesus Christ, your well-beloved Son, as he offers himself in sacrifice. Graciously receive this offering on my behalf and receive all the desires, all the sentiments, all the affections, all the movements, and all the acts of this Sacred Heart. They are all mine, since he immolates himself for me and since I intend to have no other desires henceforth but his. Receive them in satisfaction for my sins and in thanksgiving for all his benefits. Graciously receive, then, all the merits of the Sacred Heart of your divine Son which I offer and grant me in return all the graces which are necessary for me, especially the grace of final perseverance. Receive them as so many acts of love, adoration and praise which I offer to your divine majesty since it is by your divine Son alone that you are worthily honored and glorified. Amen." St. Margaret Mary

## 62 | INSTITUTION OF HOLY COMMUNION

Whenever we speak of the sacrament of the Eucharist, we normally mean Holy Communion. This is correct. Although we must remember that the Holy Eucharist is already a sacrament as the Mass and remains a sacrament after Mass is offered and Holy Communion is received.

**Promise of Christ.** St. John's Gospel is the Gospel of life. This is the evangelist's theme: God who is infinite life became man in order to give us a share in his own divine life. We receive this share in God's life at Baptism, as Christ explained in the third chapter of the Gospel of John. Three chapters later Christ promised he would nourish this life in our souls by giving us his Body to eat and his own Blood to drink. We know what happened when he made this promise. Many of his disciples left him, saying, "… This is intolerable language. Who can believe it?" (Jn 6:60b).

**The Last Supper.** What he promised, Christ fulfilled on Holy Thursday night. He took bread, blessed and broke it, and gave it to his disciples, saying, "Take and eat. This is my body, which shall be given up for you." He did the same with the chalice of wine, saying, "… All of you drink of this. For this is my blood of the new covenant, which shall be shed for you" (Lk 22:20b).

In both cases, Jesus told his disciples to be nourished on what he was giving them. "Eat" and "drink," he said, after having changed what had been bread and wine into his own living flesh and blood.

Moreover, his injunction as before with instituting the Mass, was to do what he had done—now feeding them with himself—"… in remembrance of me" (Lk 22:19b). By giving the apostles the power to change bodily food into supernatural food for the world, Jesus, then, instituted the sacrament of Holy Communion.

**Reception of Holy Communion.** Centuries before Pope St. Pius X, St. Ignatius was one of the prime movers in promoting the frequent reception of Holy Communion.

There is no more salutary amendment of life that a retreatant can make than resolve to assist at Mass and receive Our Lord in Holy Communion every day.

## Maxims of the Saints

"Whenever I approached the altar for Communion, and remembered that exceeding great majesty which I had seen, and considered that it was he in the Most Holy Sacrament, and that the Lord was often pleased that I should see him in the Host, my hair would stand on end and I would feel completely annihilated. O my Lord, if you did not cloak your greatness, who would dare to come so often to the union of such foulness and wretchedness with such great majesty." St. Teresa of Avila

"Nowhere do we find our Savior more tender or more loving than here where he, so to speak, annihilates himself and reduces himself to food in order to penetrate our souls and unite himself to the hearts of his friends." St. Francis de Sales

"Holy Communion is the shortest and surest way to heaven."
St. Pius X

| 63 | INSTITUTION OF THE REAL PRESENCE |

We reserve our meditation on the Real Presence after reflecting on the Mass and Holy Communion. Yet the Real Presence is logically prior to the Eucharist as sacrifice and communion. The reason is obvious. Christ must first be really present on earth in the Eucharist before we can intelligently speak of his offering himself in the Mass and coming to us in Communion.

Our focus here, as before, is on the *institution* of the Real Presence. What do we mean? We mean that what Christ *did* at the Last Supper, he now *is doing* every time that Mass is offered. Why? Because on Holy Thursday, he ordained the apostles as priests and thus gave them a share in his own power of transubstantiation. What had been bread and wine becomes the Body and Blood of Christ. How? By the words of consecration.

**What is the Real Presence?** The most authoritative teaching on the Real Presence is the solemn definition of the Council of Trent.

> The Body and Blood, together with the soul and divinity of our Lord Jesus Christ and, therefore, the whole Christ is truly, really and substantially contained in the sacrament of the most Holy Eucharist.

What is the Church saying? She is saying that the same identical Jesus who was conceived at Nazareth, born in Bethlehem, crucified on Calvary; who then rose from the dead on Easter Sunday and ascended into heaven on Ascension Thursday—this same Jesus, the whole Christ (*totus Christus*)—is now on earth in the Blessed Sacrament of the Eucharist.

**Why the Real Presence?** It is not hard to see why Christ is now on earth in the fullness of his humanity and divinity. He promised to be with us every day, even to the end of the world. He wanted us to profess our faith in his Incarnation, our hope in his omnipotence as the incarnate God, and our love for him, through whom all things were made. He became a man, and now dwells in our midst, no less truly, although invisibly to our bodily eyes, than he lived visibly among his contemporaries in first-century Palestine.

**How to respond to the Real Presence.** We commonly and correctly speak of Eucharistic adoration. We should, because in the Eucharist is present the whole Christ, the incarnate Son of God.

During his visible stay on earth, he received the adoration of those who believed in him. What did they believe? They believed that one who looked like a man, spoke and acted like a man, was really the living God.

We believe it is the same Jesus Christ now present in the Holy Eucharist. What do we see? Only what looks like bread and tastes like wine. What do we believe? We believe that this is no longer bread and wine, but Jesus Christ, the man who received his humanity from his mother Mary, but who is the Second Person of the Trinity who existed from all eternity.

Adoration, therefore, is the primary response of our faith to the Real Presence.

But that is only the foundation. On this worship of adoration we should build the whole edifice of the spiritual life.

- We should express our love for him since he is now on earth as the proof of his love for us.
- We should ask him for what we need, since he promised to give us everything that we ask for in his name.
- We should talk with him since that is why he is present. He wants us to be present too by communicating with him our deepest thoughts and receiving from him the illuminations and inspirations that only he can confer.
- We should not hesitate to ask him to work miracles now as he had performed wonders during his visible stay in Palestine. All that it takes is faith on our part: faith in his Incarnation, faith in his Real Presence, and faith in his power to do what is humanly impossible because he is the Almighty One.

## Maxims of the Saints

"The frequent visits to Jesus Christ in the sacrament of the altar is a great help to the souls that love him.

"That his absence from them might not be an occasion of forgetting him, this most sweet spouse, before his departure from this world left, as memorial of his love, this most holy sacrament, in which he himself remained.

"If he were to come to your church once a year and remain only for a single day, surely all would contend with one another in paying homage to him, and remaining in his loving company. And will you leave him alone and visit him so seldom, because in order to see you more frequently in his presence, he, in his goodness remains continually with you?" St. Alphonsus Liguori

"I need nothing in this world in order to be happy. I only need to see Jesus in heaven, whom I now see and adore on the altar with the eyes of faith." St. Dominic Savio

# 22

# Gethsemani, Annas, and Caiaphas

Sᴛ. Iɢɴᴀᴛɪᴜs ᴅᴇᴠᴏᴛᴇs ᴏɴᴇ ᴍᴇᴅɪᴛᴀᴛɪᴏɴ ᴇᴀᴄʜ to Christ's agony in the Garden, his being seized and taken to the high priest Annas, and his being sent to Caiaphas, son-in-law of Annas and his successor as high priest of Jerusalem.

These three meditations cover the whole sequence of Christ's passion as plotted by his own people. They did all they could to destroy him and then turned him over to the civil authorities to execute their murderous plan.

### 64 | THE AGONY IN THE GARDEN OF GETHSEMANI

The actual agony of Jesus in the Garden of Olives is narrated only by the first three evangelists.

**Jesus goes to Mt. Olivet to pray.** After the Last Supper and the institution of the Eucharist, Jesus took his eleven disciples to Mt. Olivet, where he was accustomed to pray. But he wanted to make two further decisions. He would leave eight of the eleven at the entrance to the garden while taking three of his chosen disciples closer to himself. Then he would further separate even from these three to be alone in prayer with his heavenly Father.

Christ could not be more emphatic in teaching us the value of periodically separating ourselves "from the crowd" and spending some time alone in prayerful communion with God. The Savior began his public ministry in this way, and he would close his mortal stay on earth in the same way.

**Not my will but thine be done.** Taking Peter, James, and John with him, Jesus told them to wait here and watch with him. He went off by himself to pray. These are the same three whom he had invited to witness his transfiguration. They were now to witness his humiliation.

Christ prayed three times, repeating the same prayer. "Abba, Father," he said, "all things are possible to you. Remove this chalice from me; yet not my will but thine be done" (Lk 22:42).

This is the clearest revelation of Christ's true humanity. He instinctively shrank from the sufferings he was about to undergo and the prevision of so many sinners rejecting his grace in the centuries to come. Yet his deliberate and free human will never hesitated. It was totally submissive to the divine will of his Father.

We, too, are not to be surprised at our natural reluctance to undergo pain. But that is why we have a free will—to surrender to the will of God. And the more demanding his will on us, the more generous we are in giving in to him.

**The bloody sweat.** Only St. Luke, the angelic evangelist, physician, and disciple of the converted Saul, relates:

- The angelic visitation of his Savior in his agony, "... to strengthen him" (Lk 22:43b).
- The falling into an agony. *Agonia* is the strongest word for extreme suffering in the Greek language in which St. Luke was inspired to write his Gospel.
- The sweating of blood which poured down on the ground. St. Ignatius adds that, "This supposes that his garments were saturated with blood."

We get some idea of how precious is the blood of Christ since it was out of love for us that he underwent his agony. The intensity of his interior pain indicates the intensity of his merciful love.

## Maxims of the Saints

"By reflecting beforehand on tribulation and embracing it with patience, we form to ourselves an idea of it not as an evil but as a good conducive to eternal life. Thus the premeditation takes from us the fear of the evil that the tribulation excites. This has been the practice of the saints. They have embraced crosses long before they happened, and thus they have found themselves prepared to bear them in peace when they have come suddenly upon them." St. Alphonsus Liguori

"Patient endurance is the perfection of charity." St. Augustine

## 65 | JUDAS, ANNAS, AND PETER

While Christ was still speaking to his sleeping disciples in the Garden of Olives, the crowd of Christ's Jewish enemies came rushing in. They were led by Judas Iscariot.

**The kiss of Judas.** The first three evangelists identify "one of the Twelve." He gave the crowd this sign, "... Whomever I kiss, that is he. Lay hold of him..." (Mk 14:44b). "... Do you betray the Son of Man with a kiss?" (Lk 22:48b). The word "Judas," has since become a synonym for "traitor" in the languages of all nations.

Our concern should be to remain faithful to Christ. The more gifted and influential are his followers, the more Satan tempts them to betray their Master.

**Jesus before Annas.** Jesus was brought before the Sanhedrin, the highest Jewish court that had jurisdiction in Judaea. Among its members were the chief priests.

Annas, father-in-law of Caiaphas, was the ex-high priest. Though deposed some years earlier, he had great authority in the Sanhedrin. Here was, as we would say, a defrocked cleric, presiding over a mock trial at which false witnesses were bribed to testify against the Savior. When Jesus professed to be the

Messiah, Annas had the Sanhedrin declare, "... He is liable to death" (Mk 14:64b).

This is the first verdict against Jesus because he professed to be both the Messiah and the Son of God. He did not satisfy the Messianic expectations of his contemporaries; nor has he satisfied many of them ever since.

**Peter's denial.** All four evangelists give the account of Peter's three denials of Jesus. Each time he was asked by someone if he was not one of his disciples. A combination of human respect, fear, and cowardice got the upper hand. Not only did he deny that he even knew Jesus but, "He began to curse, and to swear, 'I do not even know the man you are talking about!'" (Mk 14:71). After the third denial, the cock crowed, and Peter caught sight of Jesus looking at him. He broke down and wept bitterly.

As with Judas, another apostle disowned the Savior. But Peter, unlike Judas, repented and went on to become the first bishop of Rome. In God's providence, this was to reassure the faithful that the authority of the vicar of Christ derives from Christ himself.

### Maxims of the Saints

"When anyone makes jest of you, remember Our Lord... Let us now emulate him and so we shall be enabled even to be delivered from all insults. For it is not the insulter that gives effect to acts of insult and makes them biting but he who is little in soul and is pained by them."   St. John Chrysostom

"What was the life of Christ but a perpetual humiliation?"

St. Vincent de Paul

## 66 | JESUS BEFORE CAIPHAS

St. John is the only evangelist who narrates the trial of Jesus before the high priest Caiaphas. It had been Caiaphas who told the Jews it was expedient that one man should die for the people. But, as the evangelist had said earlier, Caiaphas said more than he realized. He was divinely inspired to say this because he was the high priest.

**God's ways are not our ways.** When Caiaphas said it was necessary for one man to die for the people, he had in mind the preservation of Israel as a nation. Jesus was a threat to the political survival of the Jewish people. But in God's providence the death of Jesus was the mysterious means of redeeming the human race.

All that Christ's enemies were doing to him, including his crucifixion, was part of God's design for the salvation of humanity. He used the malice of human beings to accomplish his own divine purpose.

**Dialogue between Christ and Caiaphas.** We are not told exactly what Caiaphas asked Jesus except that he questioned him about his disciples and his teaching. Jesus would not give him a direct answer. Instead he asked Caiaphas, "Why do you question me? Question those who have heard what I said."

At which, one of the attendants struck Jesus a blow, saying, "Is that the way to answer the high priest?" To which Jesus reacted, "… If I have spoken ill, bear witness to the evil; but if well, why do you strike me?" (Jn 18:23b). This is a powerful lesson to us. We may, and even should, defend ourselves against injustice when not to do so would jeopardize our work for the Lord.

### Maxims of the Saints

"Ah, my brother, you are mistaken, you are mistaken, if you suppose that there is ever a time when the Christian does not suffer persecution." St. Jerome

"It is to the humble-minded that Christ belongs, not to those who exalt themselves above his flock. The scepter of the divine majesty, the Lord Jesus Christ, did not, for all his power, come clothed in boastful pomp and overweening pride, but in a humble frame of mind." Pope St. Clement I

# 23

## Pilate, Herod, and Condemnation of Jesus

THE JEWISH ENEMIES OF CHRIST were legally unable to proceed any further. Their own Sanhedrin had passed judgment. In fact, they had already decided on putting Jesus to death. If they had been able to do so, they would have executed him long ago.

This deserves to be emphasized. The preaching of Christ, his claim to being the long-awaited Messiah, and worst of all, his saying that he and the Father are one—all of this had accumulatively convinced the Scribes, Pharisees, and Sadducees that he must be silenced by execution.

However, because the Romans held Palestine under their political control, Christ's opponents knew they could do nothing without Rome's authorization. That is why we have the strange sequence: first Annas and Caiaphas; then Pilate and Herod; and back to Pilate, who passed the final sentence on Jesus.

## 67 | JESUS BROUGHT BEFORE PILATE

The Roman procurator of Judaea was appointed by Emperor Tiberius. Several times during his administration there had been turbulent demonstration by the Jews when their religious traditions were violated. These demonstrations were reported to the emperor who was irritated. Pilate was therefore anxious to appease the Jews so that no further Judaean unrest was reported to Rome. This was the political situation when Pilate was confronted by the angry delegation of priests and Pharisees demanding the death of Jesus.

**The accusations against Jesus.** There were three main charges which the Jews brought against Jesus. "... We have found this man," they claimed, "perverting our nation, and forbidding the payment of taxes to Caesar, and saying that he is Christ the king" (Lk 23:2b).

All the charges were political in order to sway Pilate to condemn Jesus. Pilate then asked him whether he was a king. This occasioned Jesus making a solemn profession of his kingship. It is a synthesis of our faith. "... My kingdom," he declares, "is not of this world..." (Jn 18:36b).

Behind this statement rests everything in Christianity. We believe that Christ is king of an eternal kingdom, that our destiny is not on earth but in heaven. This was precisely why the priests and Pharisees hated Christ. They expected a Messiah who would establish Israel as an earthly kingdom. When Jesus disappointed them, they decided to destroy him.

**Pilate admits Christ's innocence.** The actual sequence was that Jesus told Pilate, "I have come into the world to bear witness to the truth." To which Pilate responded with the question, "What is truth?" Immediately after, Pilate went outside to the crowd of Jews and told them. "I find no guilt in him" (Jn 18:37-38).

If only Pilate had held firm. But the mob knew his weakness. They persisted in charging Jesus with "stirring up the people," which was the last thing Pilate wanted to hear. So, to placate the frenzied crowd, he offered them the choice between Barabbas, a notorious criminal, and Christ.

**Choice of Barabbas.** The evangelists Matthew and Mark tell us that the chief priests and the elders persuaded the crowd to ask for Barabbas.

Three times Pilate tries to reason with the crowd, and three times they shout, "... Crucify him" (Mk 15:13b).

This is an object lesson for all times. When God became man and told his contemporaries who he was only a handful believed in him. The main reason was that the professed religious leaders were really misleaders of the people. The need for humble and courageous religious leadership has not lessened but increased in the twenty centuries since the time of Christ.

**Maxims of the Saints**

"Fortitude is the love which dreads no hardship, not even death."

**St. Augustine**

"To desire to share in the kingdom—of our spouse Jesus Christ —and to enjoy it, and yet not be willing to have any part in his dishonors and trials, is ridiculous." **St. Teresa of Avila**

## 68 | CHRIST BEFORE HEROD

Herod Antipas was the son of Herod the Great who was responsible for the slaughter of the Holy Innocents. Because of Herod Antipas' devious methods, Jesus referred to him as "the fox." He was the one who had John the Baptist beheaded. He was curious about Jesus. When Pilate sent the Savior to him, "he was hoping to see some miracle done by him."

**The meeting with Herod.** Only St. Luke recounts the meeting with Herod. But not one word is recorded of what Herod said. We are told that "he put many questions to him, but he made no answer" (Lk 23:9).

Christ's silence before Herod was eloquent. Pilate sent Jesus to the tetrarch of Galilee to ingratiate himself with the Jews. Herod is not willing to listen to what Jesus might have told him. The Word of God does not waste its speech on stubborn ears.

**Accusations and mockery.** All the while that Jesus stood before Herod, "the chief priests and Scribes were standing by, accusing him." It was simply a gesture of hatred. Herod has no authority over Jesus. But Christ's enemies took this occasion once more to vent their hatred of Jesus.

Herod's pride went one step further. Along with his soldiers he mocked the Savior, treating him with contempt. The capstone of ridicule is to clothe Jesus in a bright robe, and send him back to Pilate.

**Friendship in evil.** As a result of Pilate's gesture in sending Jesus to Herod, the governor and tetrarch became friends. "Whereas previously they had been at enmity with each other" (Lk 23:12), their friendship was bought at the price of mutual crime.

### Maxims of the Saints

"If pride is the beginning of all sin, how should the swelling of pride be cured had not God vouchsafed to humble himself? Let man blush to be proud, seeing that God has humbled himself."

St. Augustine

"The lesson proposed to us in the mystery of our redemption is the humility of God." St. Benedict

## 69 | CONDEMNATION OF JESUS

The two sins that stand out in the condemnation of Jesus are hatred and cowardice.

**Hatred rooted in envy.** Pope St. Clement I, writing in the first century, teaches that envy was at the root of the hatred that finally brought Christ to his death. He was envied by the proud Jewish leaders who saw themselves ignored while Jesus was loved and admired.

**Scourging, crowning with thorns, and mockery.** In the Sorrowful Mysteries of the Rosary the sequence is: the Agony in the Garden, the Scourging, the Crowning with Thorns, the Way of the Cross, and the Crucifixion. This is the order of events during Christ's passion, as narrated in the Gospels.

In Roman law scourging was a penalty inflicted on slaves. There were two kinds of scourging: either unto death or as a preliminary to some form of execution. Christ's scourging was preliminary to his crucifixion. It was painful in the extreme. The flesh would be torn to the bone, and the loss of blood alone could be fatal.

The Crowning with Thorns was an invention of the Roman soldiers. They used this to ridicule Christ's claims to being king. To dramatize the mockery, they

- put the crown of thorns on his head;
- stripped him and clothed him in a royal purple cloak;
- bent the knee before him in homage;
- kept striking his thorn-crowned head with a reed;
- put a reed in his hands in imitation of a scepter; and
- kept coming up to him and saying, "Hail, King of the Jews" (Mt 27:29; Mk 15:17-19; Jn 19:2-3).

No wonder the church's saints have taught that Christ's crowning with thorns was especially in reparation for our sins of pride.

**Sentence of Pilate.** All the evidence shows that Pilate finally condemned Christ to death only for fear of the Jews. St. John best brings out how Pilate, though weak in will, was mentally convinced of the Savior's innocence. In fact, most of Christ's dialogue during his passion was with Pilate.

Fearing a riot, Pilate "… took water and washed his hands in sight of the crowd saying, 'I am innocent of the blood of this just man; see to it yourselves.' At which the crowd shouted, 'His blood be on us and on our children'" (Mt 27:24b-25).

Among the Jews, when the judge washed his hands, this meant he considered an accused person to be innocent. If the priests also thought the accused was innocent, they said a prayer, beginning with, "Be merciful to thy people, Lord." After this no jury would demand a death sentence. Pilate knew of this Jewish custom. Yet the priests and people, instead of the prayer for mercy, clamored for Christ's blood.

## Maxims of the Saints

"How can it be otherwise than strange, if Christ bore such things for your sake, and you cannot endure even words? He is spit upon, and do you deck yourself with garments and rings, and if you gain not a good report from all, think life unbearable? He is insulted, bears mockings and scornful blows upon the cheek; and do you wish everywhere to be honored and not bear the reproaching of Christ? Do you not hear Paul saying, 'Be imitators of me as I also am of Christ.'" **St. John Chrysostom**

"He came to us and was despised among us, first by us, afterward with us; he taught us to be despised because he was despised; taught us to endure because he endured; taught us to suffer because he suffered." **St. Augustine**

# 24

# Way of the Cross, the Crucifixion, and Burial of Christ

THE *VIA CRUCIS* OR WAY OF THE CROSS DEVOTION begins with Christ's condemnation by Pilate and ends with his burial in the tomb. Anyone making the Spiritual Exercises could not make a more practical decision of piety than to make the Stations or Way of the Cross every day.

Today's meditations are grounded in the Gospels. All four evangelists describe what occurred, and they are very detailed in their description. This is not surprising once we realize that from Pilate's court to Calvary the most significant events in world history took place.

| 70 | THE WAY OF THE CROSS |

The way of the cross began the moment Jesus was condemned by Pilate. Immediately the Roman soldiers "... took Jesus and led him away to crucify him" (Jn 19:16b).

**Publicity of the way of the cross.** The Roman custom was to give the execution of criminals the greatest possible publicity. We know from St. Luke's account of Pentecost that in Palestine at the time were people from every nation under heaven. All had come to eat the Paschal Lamb in Jerusalem. And for the first and last time in Jewish history they were about to witness the sacrifice of the Lamb of God. They were pressing across the town to make the last preparations for the feast of the Passover. Some were looking for lodging, others for a victim, and all were in the festive mood to commemorate the deliverance of the Israelites from Egypt.

They were brought to a stand by this stream of rioters, crying for death as Jesus was carrying his cross to Calvary.

The timing of everything was divinely arranged. The Jewish historian Josephus estimated that upwards of a million Jews would come to Jerusalem for the Passover. Christ planned that his *Via Crucis* would be witnessed by countless people. This was, after all, the fulfillment of all the centuries of Messianic prophecies.

**Simon of Cyrene and the women.** According to law the condemned criminal was to carry his own cross. Jesus evidently needed help. So the soldiers "... forced a passerby, Simon of Cyrene,... to take up his cross" (Lk 23:26b). Tradition tells us that Simon helped Jesus part of the way but that the Savior fell several times while carrying the cross. His humanity could not have been more evident than during this ordeal.

St. Luke tells us that there was a great crowd of people following Jesus. Among the crowd was a group of women who were "... wailing and lamenting him. Jesus turned to them and told them they should not be weeping for him but for themselves and their children" (Lk 23:27b-28). He then foretold the destruction of Jerusalem. This occurred in A.D. 70, after a siege of 143 days in which some six hundred thousand Jews perished, many by crucifixion. The Emperor Titus razed its buildings and destroyed its Temple. It is believed that the scene of Pentecost and the Last Supper was spared and became the first Christian Church.

**The title on the cross.** Although we speak of the title on the cross, it was actually to be a tablet describing the nature of the crime. St. John gives the full inscription, "... Jesus the Nazarean, THE KING OF THE JEWS" (Jn 19:19b). The chief priests immediately recognized the shameful reproach to themselves implied in the title. So they warned Pilate to change it to, "... this man said: I am King of the Jews" (Jn 19:21b, JB). Pilate refused. Thus the inscription became a title of condemnation for those who rejected their Messianic King and God.

### Maxim of St. Teresa of Avila

"Take up that cross.... In stumbling, in falling with your spouse, do not withdraw from the cross or abandon it. Consider carefully the fatigue with which he walks and how much greater his trials are to those trials you suffer, no matter how great you may want to paint them and no matter how much you grieve over them."

| 71 | THE CRUCIFIXION OF OUR LORD JESUS CHRIST |

St. Ignatius devotes only one formal meditation to Christ's actual death on Calvary. But he provides for spending "more time on the passion."

Our plan is to concentrate on the seven last words of the Savior on Calvary.

"... Father, forgive them; they do not know what they are doing..." (Lk 23:34). Christ knew that those responsible for his death were guilty. Yet he begged his Father to forgive them because they did not fully realize that they were committing deicide. The lesson for us is to pray for those who do us wrong and ask God to have mercy on those who sin against us.

"This day you shall be with me in paradise." One of the thieves crucified with Christ believes in his divinity and asked the Savior to remember him—"when you come into your kingdom." He also rebuked the unrepentant thief, because "we are receiving what our deeds deserved" (Lk 23:39-43). All that God

172 / *Retreat with the Lord*

asks of us is to admit our wrongdoing and beg forgiveness for having offended him.

**"... Woman, behold your son.... Behold your mother"** (Jn 19:26b-27a). In these words Our Lord declared Our Lady's spiritual motherhood of the human race and our responsive love of her in return. Thus we may say that Christ was making his will here and left his dearest possession on earth as a legacy to the apostles, to the Church, and to all the faithful. In these words Jesus was identifying Mary as Mother of the Church.

**"... My God, my God, why are you forsaking me?"** (Mk 15:34b). These were not the words of despair, nor do they imply that the Father was literally abandoning Jesus on the cross. They are the opening words of Psalm 21 in which are foretold the excruciating sufferings of the Messiah. This same psalm foretells the victory over spiritual death that Christ's physical death will bring to a sinful world.

**"... I thirst"** (Jn 19:28b). Certainly Jesus was thirsty to the point of death, and his body was being drained of life-sustaining water. But centuries of spiritual reflection has also seen in this cry of the Savior his deep desire to be loved by those for whom he was being crucified.

**"... It is consummated..."** (Jn 19:30b). In these words Jesus tells his Father that he has completed the mission given to him. He is also telling us that he has done everything that he could do to merit the graces of our salvation. The rest is up to us. We should have one towering hope in life: to be able to say with Christ that, "It is consummated," meaning that with his grace we have done everything we could to cooperate in his redemptive mission of saving souls.

**"... Father, into your hands I commend my spirit..."** (Lk 23:46b). These were the last recorded words of the Savior before he died. In this statement, he is saying many things:

- That he is laying down his life willingly. It is not mere resignation to the will of his Father. It is a perfectly voluntary offering of his human life as a sacrifice for the redemption of the human family.

- That he is surrendering his soul to the Father so that his body would die. Christ's divinity was never separated from either his body or his soul. But the separation of soul from body caused his death.

We are being told to follow Christ's example: always to commend our spirit into the hands of the heavenly Father. When our soul leaves the body, this will simply be the last opportunity we have of doing what we have been doing all through our mortal lives, surrendering ourselves to the will—or hands—of God.

## Maxim of St. Cyril of Jerusalem

"Let us not be ashamed of the cross of Christ. But even though another hide it, you seal it openly on your brow that the demons, seeing the royal sign, may tumble and flee away. Make this sign when eating and drinking, when sitting, lying down, rising, speaking, or walking; in a word, on every occasion."

## 72 | DEATH AND BURIAL OF CHRIST

The moment Christ died, a flood of miracles took place: the curtain of the temple was torn in two from top to bottom; the earth quaked; the rocks were split in pieces; the tombs were opened and many bodies of the holy ones appeared to people in Palestine. Even the pagan centurion professed, "... Truly this man was the Son of God" (Mk 15:39b).

**The pierced heart.** Crucifixion of itself did not cause death. That is why the Romans would burn the crucified criminals, kill them with a lance, or allow them to die of hunger. According to Jewish law, the criminal who was hanged on the cross to increase his disgrace had to be taken down and buried before evening. The Jews appealed to this law and asked Pilate to break the bones of the criminals and thus kill them.

The piercing of Christ's side by the soldier's lance is the revealed origin of devotion to the Sacred Heart. Thus the heart of Jesus was laid bare, we may say, as the seat of love, the hidden mainspring of divine life which he shared with those who believe in him, the source of all virtues and merits. It was the last shedding of his blood for us.

Ever since Calvary the devotion to the Sacred Heart has become the synthesis of our worship of Jesus Christ as incarnate Love.

**The pieta.** Pilate again enters the picture. He was asked by Joseph of Arimathea to allow Christ's body to be taken down from the cross and buried. To make sure that Jesus was dead, Pilate sent for the centurion in charge of the crucifixion, who assured the governor that Jesus was truly dead.

Taken down from the cross, tradition tells us that Mary received the body of her Son on her lap. She had held him in her arms as a child. Now his lifeless body was laid on her knees as the price of our salvation.

**The burial guard.** The evangelists Matthew and Mark identify Mary Magdalen as also being at the tomb where Jesus was buried. She and the other women "saw where he was laid" (Mt 27:61; Mk 15:47).

But Christ's enemies were afraid. They remembered he had foretold his resurrection. Although they did not believe it, they feared that some of the disciples might steal the body from the tomb and then claim that Jesus had risen from the dead. So the day after the burial, the chief priests and the Pharisees went in a body to Pilate. They told him that Jesus said "... After three days I shall rise again" (Mt 27:63b, JB). Would he place a guard at the tomb until the third day? No, he says, "... You have a guard; guard it as well as you know how" (Mt 27:65b). They not only hired a guard but sealed the tomb with a stone.

Thus the credibility of Christ's resurrection was strengthened. And once again God used the evil designs of men to further his own cause.

## Maxims of the Saints

"Neither the kingdoms of this world nor the bounds of the universe have any use for me. I would rather die for Jesus Christ than rule the last reaches of the earth." **St. Ignatius of Antioch**

"From this hell upon earth there is no escape save through the grace of the Savior Jesus Christ, our God and Lord. The very name Jesus shows this, for it means savior; and he saves us especially from passing out of this life into a more wretched and eternal state which is rather a death than a life." **St. Augustine**

"If you seek an example of contempt for earthly things, follow him, the King of kings and Lord of lords, in whom are the treasures of wisdom, and see him on the cross, despoiled, derided, spat upon, scourged, crowned with thorns, served with gall and hyssop, dead." **St. Thomas Aquinas**

# FOURTH WEEK

# Introduction to the Fourth Week

## The Resurrection and Ascension of
## Our Lord Jesus Christ

ST. IGNATIUS WAS NOT A SPECULATOR on the spiritual life. He was eminently practical. He was also very factual.

It is not surprising, then, that the fourth week of the Exercises should concentrate on the historical data of the New Testament. One meditation after another follows the sequence of events which took place from Easter Sunday morning to Ascension Thursday inclusive.

It is also not surprising that the last formal meditation of the fourth week should be on the Contemplation to Attain the Love of God, where Ignatius insists that "love should manifest itself in deeds rather than in words."

It is finally not surprising that the fourth week has a closing explanation on the Three Methods of Prayer. It was only fitting that those making the Exercises should be provided with some definite ways on how to pray. After all, the Exercises are to be a prelude to a lifetime of prayer. To achieve this we need direction. This is the purpose of the Ignatian "Three Methods of Prayer" which conclude the Spiritual Exercises.

There are several reasons why the closing week of the retreat is on the Resurrection and Ascension of Our Lord.

- This is the logic of the Gospels. They begin with Christ's conception in the womb of Mary, and they end with his bodily ascension into heaven.
- Our following of Christ here on earth is to be crowned, as was his life, with our bodily resurrection from the grave and final uniting with him for all eternity.
- Since we have served God in body and soul, we are to be rewarded, as was Christ, with our bodies and souls glorified in heaven.
- The credibility of our faith in Christ depends on the historicity of his resurrection. As St. Paul tells us, if Christ be not risen from the dead, our faith is in vain. So also would be our hope and charity, which rest on that faith as their foundation, since we cannot reasonably hope to obtain or selflessly love what we are not absolutely sure is true.

# 25

# The Risen Christ Appears to Our Lady, Mary Magdalen, and the Holy Women

IT IS NOT ST. IGNATIUS BUT THE EVANGELISTS who feature the role of women in the resurrection of Christ.

Matthew, Mark, Luke, and John begin their narrative of the resurrection with the women at the grave on early Easter Sunday morning. Matthew, Mark, and John describe Christ's appearance to Mary Magdalen. Matthew, Mark, and Luke record the angels speaking to the women at the empty grave. Matthew and Luke describe how the women inform the apostles. A total of over forty verses in the Gospels feature the role of women at the resurrection of the Savior.

Some reasons for this are obvious. The women who followed Christ were more ready to believe in him during his public ministry and passion and also after his resurrection from the dead. Their love for the Savior was more openly manifest.

This has many implications but especially one: Christianity needs the loving faith of women believers as a condition for its growth and stability.

## 73 | CHRIST APPEARS TO HIS MOTHER

It is not mere pious fancy that the risen Christ first appeared to his mother. It is well founded in the Church's tradition, and more than one doctor of the Church affirms this as an unquestionable fact of history.

St. Ignatius himself says, "Though it is not mentioned explicitly in the Scripture, it must be considered as stated when Scripture says that he appeared to many others. For Scripture supposes that we have understanding, as it is written, 'Are you also without understanding?'"

**Appearance to the souls of the just.** In the language of the Exercises, "after Christ expired on the cross, his body remained separated from the soul but always united with his divinity. His soul, likewise united with his divinity, descended into hell. There he sets free the souls of the just, then comes to the sepulchre, and rising, appears in body and soul to his Blessed Mother."

Christ descended in soul to the Limbo of the Fathers, as it is called, in order to reassure the faithful departed of the Old Law that their redemption had been accomplished. They appreciated this assurance because some of them had waited centuries, anticipating the day when the promised Savior of humanity would expiate the sins of the world.

**Jesus meets his mother.** Before appearing to anyone else, the risen Savior comes to see his Blessed Mother. St. Ignatius recommends that I see "the house of Our Lady, I will note its different parts, and also her room, her oratory," and the like.

Mary's faith in the resurrection of her Son never wavered. That is why over the centuries Saturdays have been specially dedicated to Our Lady. They are variously called, "Mary Day" or "Faith Day." The first Holy Saturday she alone never doubted that her Son's promise of raising himself from the grave would be realized. She firmly believed that, as he said, like Jonah the prophet he would come out of the earth alive in his glorified humanity.

**Mary's faith rewarded.** Unlike her divine Son, Mary had to live by faith. Unlike him she did not possess the Beatific Vision during her mortal stay on earth. She therefore deserved to have her deep faith rewarded by being the first witness of his resurrection.

The body in which Christ appeared to his mother was the body he had received from her. Thus the annunciation and the resurrection are complementary. The Second Person of the Holy Trinity took on our human nature and assumed a human body for two basic reasons:

- In order to be able to suffer and die on the cross for our redemption.
- In order to be able to rise from the dead and thus, through his humanity, to commemorate the graces of Calvary until the end of time.

Mary was the first recipient of these graces of her risen Son, even as she was to become the divinely chosen mediatrix of these graces, from him, through her, to all of us.

### Maxim of St. Ignatius

"After Christ expired on the cross, his body remained separated from the soul, but always united with the divinity. The soul like-wise united with the divinity, descended into hell (the Limbo of the Fathers). There he sets free the souls of the just, then comes to the sepulchre, and rising, appears in body and soul to his blessed Mother."

| 74 | CHRIST APPEARS TO MARY MAGDALEN |

Among the evangelists the most detailed account of Our Lord's appearing to Mary Magdalen is given by St. John. This is not surprising since John is so explicit in identifying Mary Magdalen as being on Calvary when Jesus was crucified. However, St. Ignatius concentrates in this meditation on the Gospel of St. Mark. The holy women, the angel, and the risen Savior are the speakers quoted in this narrative.

**Conversation of the three Marys.** Very early on Easter Sunday morning, "... Mary Magdalen, Mary the mother of James, and Salome [went] to the tomb" (Mk 16:1b). They knew that the Pharisees had sealed the tomb with a huge stone. They seem not to have known that there were also guards stationed at the tomb.

On their way, they asked themselves, "Who will roll the stone back from the entrance of the tomb for us?"

They were not expecting to find the tomb empty. On the contrary, they thought Christ's body was still in the tomb. As St. Mark explained, they "... bought spices with which to go and anoint him" (Mk 16:1b, JB). Thus they wanted to show their deep love for Jesus whom they did not expect to have risen from the dead.

**Message of the angel.** The women entered the empty tomb, from which the stone had been removed. Inside the tomb, they saw a young man seated at the right side. They were amazed.

He told them, "... Do not be terrified. You are looking for Jesus of Nazareth, who was crucified. He has risen, He is not here. Behold the place where they had laid him" (Mk 16:6b).

The angel in human form gave the women instructions. "Go tell his disciples and Peter that he goes before you into Galilee; there you shall see him as he told you" (Mk 16:7).

They had forgotten the prophecy that Jesus had made that he would raise himself from the dead. He was back in his native province of Galilee.

**Jesus appears to Mary Magdalen.** As mentioned before, the evangelist John is most extensive in his narrative of Christ's appearance to Mary Magdalen.

One of John's purposes for writing the fourth Gospel was to attest to the historical fact of Christ's true divinity and true humanity. In Christ's conversation with Mary Magdalen, he told her to go to the apostles and tell them, "I am ascending to my Father and your Father, to my God and your God." Thus the Savior distinguishes between his two natures. As the only begotten Son of the eternal Father, he speaks of God as "my Father" (Jn 20:17). As the Word become flesh he is speaking of his human nature which he has in common with us, and therefore he speaks for all of us in addressing God as "our Father."

St. Mark makes a telling reference to this Mary Magdalen being the same one "... out of whom he had cast seven demons" (Mk 16:9b).

In the centuries of the Church's history, converted sinners have been among the most ardent lovers of Jesus Christ and the most zealous apostles of his kingdom. In fact, Mary Magdalen has the unique title of *apostola* (feminine gender) *apostolorum* (masculine gender), that is, "the apostle of the apostles."

### Maxim of St. Gregory I

"Mary Magdalen had been a notorious sinner. Loving the Truth, she cleansed her sins with her tears. Unlike the disciples who fled, she did not flee. In the great strength of her love, she came to the tomb of the Lord."

## 75 | CHRIST APPEARS TO THE HOLY WOMEN

St. Ignatius has a separate meditation on Christ's appearance to the two Marys of James and Salome.

**Fear and joy to announce Christ's resurrection.** The first evangelist relates that the women who came to the sepulchre and were instructed by the angel "... departed from the tomb in fear and joy and ran to tell the disciples" (Mt 28:8b).

This combination of fear and joy is understandable. The women were afraid of the unknown. They were frightened by the humanly unexplainable events they had just witnessed: an empty tomb where Christ's body was buried just two days before, and an angel telling them that the Savior was risen. But they were also very happy to learn that Jesus of Nazareth, who they knew was crucified, had risen from the dead. It was the joy of knowing that he was once more bodily in their midst.

**Jesus meets them on the way.** Having been faithful in following out the angel's directive, the women have their faith rewarded by Christ meeting them en route to the apostles.

He greeted them, "Hail," even as the angel Gabriel greeted

Mary at the annunciation. They were overjoyed, embraced his feet, and worshiped him (Mt 28:17).

**Mission of the holy women.** Christ repeats the instruction of the angel at the tomb. Again, he specifies Galilee as the place where not only the apostles but also the holy women will be privileged to see Jesus.

It is highly significant that Christ should have not once but twice directed dedicated women to go and announce his resurrection to the apostles. Only the apostles were to be the foundation on which Christ built his Church. And yet it was devoted women whose great love for Jesus inspired them—and not the apostles—to come to the tomb at early dawn on Easter Sunday. We may reemphasize what was said before. The faith of the Church, including the Church's leaders, depends in large measure on the selfless fidelity of loving Marys. As goes the loving faith of women in the Church, so goes the Church in every age of her history and every place of her existence.

## Maxims of the Saints

"How tenderhearted and inclined to sympathy is womankind!"
St. John Chrysostom

"If women were worthy to be believed, why did the disciples not believe the holy women? We must give thought to the gracious providence of our Lord in this incident. For this was the means used by the Lord Jesus Christ so that the female sex might be the first to announce that he had risen. Because man's fall was occasioned by womankind, man's restoration was accomplished through womankind." St. Augustine

# 26

# Appearance to Peter and the Disciples of Emmaus, the Institution of the Sacrament of Reconciliation

THE THREE MEDITATIONS FOR TODAY are among the most important of the Spiritual Exercises. They bring out three mysteries of the Catholic faith that need to be clearly understood.

- The leadership of the Apostle Peter and the primacy of Peter and his successors in the papacy.
- The need for patient endurance of the cross in the faithful following of Christ.
- The Sacrament of Reconciliation, or Penance, as the continuation of Christ's redemptive mission now on earth in reconciling sinners with a just God.

These three meditations are closely related. Without the papal primacy, the Church's superhuman stability could not have been maintained. Without the faithful following of Christ in carrying the cross, Christianity would be just another form of religious mythology. And without the Sacrament of Reconciliation the mission of Christ to save sinners would be only a pleasant memory or a fond hope of divine mercy.

## 76 | CHRIST APPEARS TO PETER

Once again St. Ignatius interprets sacred Scripture according to a definite purpose he has in the Spiritual Exercises.

There are two loyalties that he wants to bring home to those who make the Exercises. They are loyalty to Christ's mother and loyalty to Christ's vicar on earth, the successor of St. Peter.

To bring out the first loyalty, Ignatius makes sure we know to whom Christ first appeared on Easter Sunday: his mother Mary. To bring out the second loyalty, he concentrates on Peter as the one who, with John, first visited the empty tomb and the one of whom the other apostles said, "... The Lord has risen and has appeared to Simon" (Lk 24:34b, JB).

**The women's message followed.** In St. Luke's version Peter alone is described as going to the tomb in response to the women's report from Jerusalem. In one verse he says that "Peter arose and ran to the tomb..." (Lk 24:12a). The evangelist John says that "Peter went out, and the other disciple (John), and they went to the tomb" (Jn 20:3).

St. Ignatius' focus is on Peter to bring out the unique role that the head of the apostles had in the early Church but also to lay the foundation for the unique role that the successors of Peter would have in stabilizing and unifying the Church until the end of time.

**Peter enters the tomb.** According to the fourth evangelist, John reached the tomb before Peter. Yet John waited to allow Peter to enter the tomb first. All Catholic commentators make note of this fact. It shows how instinctively the other apostles, even the "beloved disciple," recognized Peter's leadership in the apostolic college. This is of towering importance in post-conciliar times, to realize that there is no true collegiality except under the authority of the successors of St. Peter.

**Selective appearance to Peter.** Again St. Luke, who concentrated on Peter alone as going to the tomb, recalls the statement of the other apostles, reporting to the disciples of Emmaus that "the Lord is risen indeed and has appeared to Simon" (Lk 24:34).

No details are given in the Gospels about this special appearance to Simon Peter. What should be noted, however, is the sequence of events:

- The women went to the tomb and found it empty. They were told to report this to the apostles.
- Peter (with John) ran to the tomb and found it empty but with evidence of Christ's being risen because the linen cloth in which his body had been shrouded was now "... folded in a place by itself" (Jn 20:7b).
- Peter had Christ appear to him because he responded to the women's announcement and had his faith verified by the empty tomb and its contents. As the visible head of the Church after Christ, he was among the first to witness the Savior's resurrection.

**Maxim of St. John Chrysostom**

"Peter, leader of the chair, the mouth of all the apostles, the head of that college, the ruler of the whole world, the foundation of the church, the ardent lover of Christ."

| 77 | THE DISCIPLES OF EMMAUS |

Except for one verse in St. Mark, the evangelist Luke gives us the only detailed account of what happened when Christ appeared to two disciples on their way to Emmaus.

St. Luke's extensive narrative can be explained on several counts. He was the disciple of St. Paul, the apostle of divine mercy and of the Holy Eucharist, both of which are brought out in the conversation of Christ with the Emmaus disciples. Moreover, St. Paul was the Apostle of the Gentiles since the chosen people rejected Jesus because they were looking for a Messiah who would create an earthly kingdom of Israel.

**Christ joins the disciples to Emmaus.** On Easter Sunday two of the disciples were going from Jerusalem to Emmaus while talking about Jesus. They were walking the long distance and "arguing with one another" about all that had happened over the weekend (Lk 24:14). Evidently they misunderstood the events of Holy Week.

**Jesus explains the meaning of the passion.** Without revealing his identity, Jesus first drew from the disciples what they were so sad about. They told him, "We were hoping that it was he (Jesus) who should redeem Israel...." (Lk 24:21a).

He reprimanded them, "... O foolish ones and slow of heart to believe in all that the prophets have spoken. Did not Christ have to suffer these things before entering into his glory?" (Lk 24:25b-26).

That is the key to the whole mystery of the Messiah. He was to be the Suffering Servant foretold by Isaiah, whose message to the Israelites was to place their trust in God and not in military achievements.

**Christ gives the Eucharist.** On their request, Jesus sat down to eat with the disciples. While at table he changed bread and wine into his Body and Blood. In the words of St. Ignatius, "He gave them Holy Communion. Then he disappeared. Thereupon, they returned to the disciples and told them how they recognized him in Holy Communion.

Evidently Christ did not wait one day after his resurrection to celebrate what may be called his second Mass, the first one being on Holy Thursday night.

The lesson is clear. If we are to follow Christ faithfully, we must expect to suffer like him. For this we will need the strength of mind and heart that only he can give. The principal source of this spiritual courage is the Holy Eucharist.

## Maxim of St. Augustine

"How do you think my heart rejoices when we seem to be superior to those who were walking along the road and to whom the Lord appeared? For we have believed what they did not believe. They had lost hope while we have no doubt about what caused them to waver." St. Augustine

# 78 INSTITUTION OF THE SACRAMENT OF RECONCILIATION

Christ waited until his resurrection from the dead before instituting the Sacrament of Reconciliation or Penance. This stands to reason. He had come into the world to save sinners. This meant more than meriting our salvation. It meant giving us constant access to his merciful grace of forgiveness whenever we should lose his friendship by committing mortal sin.

In his second rule for thinking with the Church, St. Ignatius states, "We should praise sacramental confession." And in his directives to the priests of his Society of Jesus, he prescribed Confession at least once a week. When we reflect on how widely Confession was neglected in the sixteenth century, we realize that for Ignatius this sacrament is not only necessary for the confident remission of grave sins, it is indispensable for growth in sanctity.

**The apostles in hiding.** The chosen disciples of Christ went into hiding after Christ's crucifixion. As explained by the evangelist John, "When it was late that same day, the first of the week, the doors where the disciples gathered had been closed for fear of the Jews..." (Jn 20:19a). They were afraid that as close followers of Jesus, they too would be hauled before the Sanhedrin and maybe even put to death. This shows how humanly weak they were, because they did not grasp the real meaning of Christ's passion and death. The Apostle Thomas was not with them. His faith seems to have been even weaker than that of the others.

**Christ gives his peace.** Three events then took place in rapid sequence:

- Christ came through the closed doors, stood before the apostles, and told them, "... Peace be with you" (Jn 20:19b).
- He then showed them the wounds in his hands and side. At the sight of this witness to Christ's identity as the crucified but now risen Savior, they rejoice.

- For the second time Jesus told the disciples, "Peace be with you…" (Jn 20:21a).

Ever since that historic Easter Sunday night, the Sacrament of Reconciliation has been known as the Sacrament of Peace. The reason is obvious. The single most common and painful source of conflict in the human heart is the sense of guilt over sin.

Correspondingly, the most powerful source of peace of heart is the assurance of reconciliation with a merciful God. This assurance is one of the great gifts of the Sacrament of Reconciliation.

**Institution of the Sacrament of Reconciliation.** It is an article of the Catholic faith that Christ instituted the Sacrament of Reconciliation or Penance on Easter Sunday when he told the apostles, "For those sins you forgive, they are forgiven; for those whose sins you retain, they are retained" (Jn 20:23, JB). What was Our Lord telling the apostles?

- He was telling them to decide in his name whose sins should be remitted.
- He was therefore saying that penitents were to confess their sins. Otherwise, how could the apostles—and their successors—be able to judge whose sins should be forgiven or retained?
- He was sharing with them the power of not only proclaiming Christ's mercy but of actually remitting the sins confessed.

All of the above is contained in Christ's injunction to the apostles, to "… Receive the Holy Spirit" (Jn 20:22b). They were receiving from Christ a share in the power of forgiving sins which he had received, as the Son of Man from his heavenly Father.

### Maxim of St. John Chrysostom

"Then when he had removed all hindrances and had established the fact of his own brilliant victory setting everything right, he finally said, 'As the Father has sent me, I also send you. You will have no difficulty at all, both by reason of the events that have already taken place and also by reason of the fact that I who send you am of exalted dignity.' By his words he was uplifting their spirits and giving indisputable proof that they could have confidence in him if they would undertake the task he was assigning.

"Moreover he was no longer asking the Father to help them but was giving them his own authority. 'For he breathed on them and said: Receive the Holy Spirit; whose sins you shall forgive, they are forgiven them; and whose sins you shall retain, they are retained.' Like a king who, as he sends out governors, gives them power to imprison and also to release from prison, so likewise in sending the disciples, he endowed them with this power."

# 27

# Thomas, the Papal Primacy, and the Command to Evangelize the Whole World

THE CLOSING THREE MEDITATIONS on the risen Christ are also the last three recorded by the evangelists. They are a synthesis of Christianity as the Word of God revealed to the world by the Word who is God become flesh and who dwells among us.

Underlying all three meditations is the necessity of faith. The naturally proud human intellect must submit to the mind of God and believe everything which he, especially as the God-man, has told us to accept on his Word.

The Apostle Thomas typifies what has been going on ever since Easter Sunday. The divinity of Christ is doubted or denied by millions who may still call themselves Christians.

The papal primacy has likewise become the scandal of those who refuse to believe that Christ had chosen Peter and his successors to be the rock on which the Savior has built his Church. It is the rock of faith by which the mysteries we believe in are the foundation of our unity as followers of Christ.

Christ's closing commission to the apostles was to make disciples of all nations. To be a disciple of Christ means many things. But most fundamentally it means the voluntary assent to Christ's teaching in humble obedience of the intellect to everything which he, who is the Truth, has revealed to us as true.

| 79 | THE APOSTLE THOMAS'
PROFESSION OF FAITH |
|----|---|

St. Ignatius devotes a whole meditation to the Apostle Thomas' refusal to believe in Christ's resurrection and his final submission to revealed truth.

Not surprisingly only St. John records the event. By the end of the first century, when the fourth Gospel was written, a variety of heresies had arisen regarding Christ's true divinity and humanity. The story of the doubting apostle, therefore, reveals how no one is exempt from the seductive pride of disbelief, not even the closest personal followers of the Savior.

**Thomas' refusal to believe.** There were two apostles missing on Easter Sunday night when Jesus appeared to them. Judas had hanged himself after betraying the Master. Thomas was unexplainably absent, although his later attitude on returning suggests that his courage had failed him after the events of Good Friday.

On returning to the upper room in Jerusalem, he not only refused to believe that Christ had risen, he laid down the conditions for believing.

We commonly speak of him as the "doubting Thomas." More accurately he should be called the "denying Thomas." Doubt is the withholding of assent; denial is the positive refusal to assent— in this case to the fact of Christ's bodily resurrection.

Nothing is more basic in Christianity than unqualified assent to everything which the church teaches has been revealed by Christ. Thomas withheld his assent to what the apostolic Church was telling him, that Jesus was truly risen. As Peter and the other apostles told him, "… We have seen the Lord!…" (Jn 20:25b).

**Christ's reprimand.** Christ might have left Thomas in his disbelief, and there would then have been one less apostle in the apostolic college. Instead, Jesus returned a week later, again through closed doors. His greeting, "… Peace be with you" (Jn 20:26b), was an affirmation of the apostles' faith made possible through the grace of Christ. Our minds are at peace when they possess the truth.

Then Jesus told Thomas, "Bring here your finger, and see my hands; and bring here your hand, and put it into my side, and be not unbelieving" (Jn 20:27).

We do not know whether Thomas actually put his finger into the Savior's pierced hands or his hand into the pierced side. Probably not.

**Profession of faith.** Thomas' reaction has become part of Christian history and our Catholic liturgy.

What did Thomas say? He said, "... My Lord and my God!" (Jn 20:28b). He spoke these words to a man named Jesus of Nazareth. He professed his faith in Jesus as his Lord and his God.

The Fathers of the Church make much of this profession of faith. It is the single most explicit, most clear, most unqualified witness of the Gospels to Christ's divinity. It is also a fact of verifiable history.

No wonder so many reputed scholars question or openly deny that the fourth Gospel was written by St. John the Apostle or claim it was of post-apostolic origin. This Gospel, from start to finish, is too explicit for the doubting Thomases of our day in its unambiguous evidence that Christ's resurrection confirms the fact of his oneness with God the Father.

Our Lord's response to Thomas says more than may be evident at first. He told the apostle, "... Because you have seen me, you have believed. Blessed are they who have not seen and yet have believed" (Jn 20:29b). Thomas should have accepted the word of the other apostles, that they had indeed seen the risen Savior. His sin was in his unwillingness to believe. We do believe with our minds. But first our wills must be disposed to believe. Otherwise the mind remains closed to any evidence that God has made a revelation and that what he tells us is true.

## Maxim of St. John Chrysostom

"Just as it is an indication of gullibility to believe easily and carelessly, so to scrutinize and examine immoderately before believing is the mark of an obstinate will. That is why Thomas is blameworthy. For he refused to believe the apostles when they said: 'We have seen the Lord,' not so much because he did not trust them as because he considered the thing an impossibility— that is, resurrection from the dead. He did not say: 'I do not believe you,' but, 'Unless I put my hand into his side, I will not believe.'

"Jesus once again stood in their midst but did not wait to be approved by Thomas or to hear from him any such conditions as he had laid down for accepting the apparition as genuine.

"After saying: 'Bring thy finger, and see my hands, and put thy hand into my side,' he added: 'and be not unbelieving but believing,' do you see that Thomas was hesitating because of his unbelief? However, this was before he had received the Spirit. Afterwards they no longer doubted but were henceforth unhesitating in their belief.

"But it was not only by these words that he reproved him, but also by his next words. For when Thomas, now fully convinced, could breathe again and cried out: 'My Lord and my God,' Christ said: 'Because thou hast seen me, thou hast believed. Blessed are they who have not seen and yet have believed.' This is indeed a proof of faith, namely, to accept what we have not seen. For 'Faith is the substance of things to be hoped for, the evidence of things that are not seen.' Moreover, Christ was here declaring that not only were his disciples blessed but also those to come after them, who would believe."

## 80  THE CONFERRAL OF THE PRIMACY

Throughout the Gospels Peter stands out as the leader among the apostles. Moreover, in St. Matthew's Gospel, Jesus promises to make Peter the rock on which he will build his Church. But it was not until the last chapter of John's Gospel that Christ actually conferred the papal primacy on Peter and his successors until the end of time.

**The miraculous draught of fish.** As so often before, Jesus worked a miracle in order to make his teaching credible. He did this by miraculously feeding the hungry multitude before his promise of giving his own flesh to eat and blood to drink to sustain our supernatural life. He did this again by raising Lazarus from the dead in order to confirm our faith in him as our resurrection and our life. He did this finally by enabling the disciples to make a miraculous catch of large fish, at his word, from the same water where they had fished all night and caught nothing. This miracle was the prelude to Christ's giving Peter and his successors in the papacy supreme authority on earth over the people of God.

**Peter comes to Christ.** St. Ignatius stresses the fact that "through this miracle, John recognizes him and says to Peter, 'It is the Lord.' St. Peter casts himself into the sea and comes to Christ" (Jn 21:7).

Call it impetuosity or the outburst of a deep love, Peter's swimming to Christ on the shore reveals both his impulsive nature and the impetus of divine grace.

Grace, we believe, builds on nature. God uses the nature we have to produce, by his grace, the person he wants to form for the extension of his kingdom.

**The primacy.** What Christ had promised, he conferred on Peter on the shore of the Sea of Tiberias.

Peter had denied Christ three times. So three times Christ asked him, "Do you love me?" (Jn 21:15-17).

But in his first question Jesus asked Peter, "Do you love me more than these do?" Why "more"? Because Peter had more love to give to Christ in expiation for his triple denial of the Master. This is a law of divine mercy. God allowed us to fail in loving him by sin in the past so that we might be more self-giving in our love for him in the future.

Each of the three denials corresponds to a distinct power of authority that Christ gave to Peter and his successors in the papacy.

- Peter and they received a mandate to feed the lambs, the youngest of Christ's flock. They were to teach revealed

truth, which alone sustains the human mind in the supernatural life.
- Peter and they were to tend the sheep of Christ's flock by
directing the wills of the faithful through laws and administration according to the will of Christ.
- Peter and they were to feed the sheep of Christ's flock with
ongoing nourishment of their souls. Their intellects are to
be fed all through life with true doctrine.

Among these truths on which Christ's flock is to be sustained
is the mystery of faith, the Real Presence of Christ in the Holy
Eucharist. Except for this faith there could be no real Mass, no
real Communion, and, we must say, no Catholic Church.

### Maxim of St. John Chrysostom

"Christ entrusted to Peter the primacy over his brethren to show
him that in the future he must have no fear because his denial
had been completely forgiven. Moreover, he did not bring up
the denial at all or find fault with him for what had happened
and said in effect: If you love me, assume responsibility for your
brethren, and now show to them the ardent love which you have
always displayed towards me and in which you have gloried. And
for the sake of the lambs lay down that life which you used to say
you would lay down for me."

## 81 | CHRIST'S FINAL COMMISSION TO THE APOSTLES

The final meditation on the risen Christ is also the closing of St.
Matthew's Gospel.

St. Ignatius emphasizes the solemnity of the event by recalling
that Christ commanded the disciples to go to Mount Tabor
where he would give them the commission that would continue
until the end of time. Ignatius also explains that Jesus sends the

apostles "throughout the world." This is the heart of the Spiritual Exercises, to inspire those who believe in Christ to propagate his teaching to the widest reaches of the globe.

**Command of Christ.** It was in Galilee that Christ was conceived when the Word of God became man and dwelt among us. It was to be a mountain in Galilee where the now glorified Christ sent out his apostles to proclaim the good news of salvation to the whole world.

Christ gave his historic sermon on a mountain where he revealed the Beatitudes. It was on Mount Calvary that he was crucified. And it was from a mountain that he proclaimed the mission that his apostles were to carry out.

**Almighty power of Christ.** When Christ said that, "… All power is given to me in heaven and on earth," he meant especially his moral power or right to command all rational creatures to obey his will (Mt 28:18b).

In making the Spiritual Exercises, we base our faith on the divinity of Christ as a key truth. What needs to be stressed, however, is that Christ's divinity gives him the right to command our wills to obey his will.

So true is this that he made this obedience the test of fidelity to his name. "If you love me," he said, "keep my commandments" (Jn 14:15).

**The obligation to evangelize.** Since the foundation of the Church, she has never ceased to proclaim the obligation to proclaim the fullness of Christ's revelation to the whole world.

Already on Christmas morning the angel told the shepherds he was bringing them good news of great joy "which shall be to all people." This mandate has never been questioned by the Catholic Church. The very term "Catholic" means universal. And part of this universality is the divine mandate to evangelize.

In our age of communication some are questioning this mandate. They claim that non-Christians are really "anonymous Christians" who should be left to their own persuasions and not be actively evangelized. This is not the teaching of Christ.

How are people to be evangelized? In three ways, and all three are essentials of evangelization.

- They are to be made "disciples." This means they are to be taught what Christ revealed so that their minds accept his teaching in humility of faith.
- They are to be baptized. This means that they are to be reborn in spirit through the waters of Baptism.
- They are to observe all the commandments which God became man to enjoin on the human race.

Then, in a simple phrase, Jesus assures his followers not to be afraid to evangelize. He told the apostles and is telling us, "... I am with you always, even to the consummation of the world" (Mt 28:20b). We have the promise of his presence with us in the Eucharist as the physical Christ and in the church as the mystical Christ. With him we can convert the whole world to his name.

### Maxim of St. Ambrose

"The Father forgives sin, just as the Son forgives; likewise also the Holy Spirit. But he bade us to be baptized in one name, that is 'in the name of the Father, and of the Son, and of the Holy Spirit.' Wonder not that he spoke of one name when there is one substance, one divinity, one majesty."

# 28

# The Bodily Ascension of Jesus Christ into Heaven

IN THE SPIRITUAL EXERCISES THE MEDITATION on the Ascension of Christ Our Lord is the last of the mysteries of the life of Our Lord. This is consistent with St. Ignatius' concentration on Christ's visible stay on earth, from the Incarnation at Nazareth to his bodily ascension into heaven.

After all, the Christ whom we are to listen to and imitate really lived on earth in sensibly perceptible form. He really talked and walked, and ate and slept, and died. He really rose from the dead, and he really left the earth as a visible man. The ascension, therefore, is part of New Testament history. It is, of course, an article of our faith and also a historical event.

As St. Ignatius saw this mystery, it has three distinct elements. Each element is not only rich in doctrinal content. It is also filled with implications for the spiritual life.

The first part of the mystery is Christ's promise to send the Holy Spirit. The second is the actual ascension. And the third is the message of the angels that Christ will return to earth in the same way that he went to heaven forty days after his resurrection.

## 82 | THE PROMISE OF THE HOLY SPIRIT

It is part of our Catholic faith that there have been two missions, or sendings, from God to the human race. The first mission was from the Father who sent his Son into the world in visible form. Jesus of Nazareth more than once spoke of his being sent by the Father, and on the cross his dying words were, "It is finished," that is, his mission of reconciling a sinful human family with the Father was accomplished.

The second mission was invisible. It took place on Pentecost Sunday, and its effects will continue for all ages and into the ageless eternity. The Second Person of the Trinity became man and ascended into heaven, as he said, so that he might send from the Father the Third Person of the Holy Trinity to bring to completion his own visible mission of humanity's redemption.

**Supernatural power.** As described by St. Luke, the evangelist of the Holy Spirit, Christ told his disciples, "I send forth among you the promise of my Father. But wait here in the city until you are clothed with power from on high" (Lk 24:49). The power that he was promising was that they and his followers until the end of time might be witnesses to him, not only in Judaea and Samaria but even "... to the ends of the earth" (Acts 1:8b).

What kind of power would they receive? Power of intellect to understand his teaching and power of will to courageously proclaim his name.

This, in fact, is precisely what the Sacrament of Confirmation gives to those who are confirmed. They receive what the Church calls "spiritual strengthening." Since apostolic times this sacrament has been compared to the first coming of the Holy Spirit on Pentecost Sunday.

**The grace of martyrdom.** In the Acts of the Apostles where Christ promised to send the Holy Spirit, the original Greek of St. Luke says that they "will be my martyrs." This is most revealing. It says exactly what kind of power the disciples were to receive. It was to be the power of witnessing to Christ—indeed, but witnessing under opposition, persecution, and under threat of physical or at least emotional death.

This is the power of both those who died a martyr's death and those who lived a martyr's life. This is the power that has sustained the Church through the first three centuries of her history, which we have come to call the Age of Martyrs.

But ours, the present century, is even more so the Age of Martyrs. More followers of Christ have shed their blood in witness to his name since 1900 than in all the previous nineteen centuries put together.

If there is one grace that everyone who makes the Spiritual Exercises should ask of God, it is the grace of martyrdom, either actually shedding one's blood for Jesus Christ or spiritually being put to death in testimony of one's faith in the Savior who died on the cross for our salvation.

**Apostolic fertility.** Surely one of the deepest paradoxes of Christianity is that the Church has actually flourished under persecution.

The Holy Spirit, whom Christ promised to send, came on Pentecost Sunday in the form of fiery tongues. This we identify as the apostolic birthday of Christianity.

The Church came into being—she was born—on Calvary. But she began to propagate on Pentecost Sunday. One short sermon of St. Peter brought several thousand converts. But that was only the beginning. So powerful was the grace of the Holy Spirit that as the Church was more opposed so much more did she grow. The early Fathers coined the expression, "The blood of martyrs is the seed of Christians" (*Sanguis Martyrum, Semen Christianarum*). Why should this be? Because the patient suffering of faithful Christians merited the conversion of their very enemies.

## Maxim of St. Augustine

"What the soul is to the body of man, the Holy Spirit is in the Body of Christ, which is the Church. The Holy Spirit does that in the whole Church which the soul does in all the members of a single body."

| **83** | THE ACTUAL ASCENT OF CHRIST |

Only Saints Mark and Luke describe Christ's actual ascent into heaven.

Mark says: "And so the Lord Jesus, after he had spoken to them, was taken up into heaven: there at the right hand of God he took his place" (Mk 16:19, JB). Luke records the ascension in both his Gospel and in the Acts of the Apostles. It is typical of the disciple of St. Paul to be very specific, even detailed in his narratives. His Gospel version is worth quoting in full. It is the closing verses of the third Gospel:

> Now he led them out towards Bethany, and he lifted up his hands and blessed them. And it came to pass as he blessed them, that he parted from them and was carried up into heaven. And they worshiped him and returned to Jerusalem with great joy. **Lk 24:50-52**

The Lucan account in the Acts is shorter but adds an important detail. Christ had just told the disciples to wait for the coming of the Spirit. "And when he had said this, he was lifted up before their eyes, and a cloud took him out of their sight" (Acts 1:9).

**The historicity of the ascension.** Certainly Christ's ascension has many religious meanings. But the first thing we need to make sure is that, like St. Ignatius, we have no doubt about the historical event.

Christ in his bodily existence spoke with physical lips. He blessed the disciples with physical hands. And he was physically lifted up from the earth, departing from the disciples in a sensibly perceptible way.

St. Luke's statement that "… a cloud took him from their sight" only emphasizes the literalness of what took place on Ascension Thursday (Acts 1:9b, JB).

Certainly Jesus did not travel bodily through millions of light years of space to reach heaven. But he was physically elevated on

Ascension Thursday. His ascension took place. It is no mere symbolism or projection of religious fantasy.

**Why the ascension?** Our Lord ascended into heaven for many reasons. But one reason was to dramatize the real distinction between heaven and earth.

What does this mean? Of course, it means that there are two different states of existence, the terrestrial and the celestial. But it means much more. It means that the human body is to have two stages of being, one on earth and the other in heaven.

After all, Christ truly merited heaven. His cooperation with divine grace won for him a heavenly reward, a reward not only in soul but in body. Why? Because during his mortal life on earth, he had cooperated in body *and* soul with the grace of his heavenly Father.

**Spiritual implications.** The obvious implication for us is that we can expect to share in Christ's dual reward if we follow his example during our mortal life here on earth. Our bodies will be in heaven with his provided we too have responded to God's will with our bodies even as he always did the will of his Father with his body.

It is of more than passing importance that our wills have power to command and direct our bodies. In the measure that we are now faithful in doing this as Christ wants us to, we are destined to join him in a blessed eternity.

## Maxim of St. Augustine

"On this day, that is, on the fortieth day after his resurrection, the Lord ascended into heaven. We did not witness his ascension, but let us believe. Those who did witness it proclaimed it and filled the entire world [with their preaching]. You know that those who witnessed it and who told us about it, the Scripture had predicted, 'There are no speeches nor languages, where their voices are not heard. Their sound has gone forth into all the earth and their words unto the ends of the world.' Hence their voices have reached us and have aroused us from sleep.

Behold this day is being celebrated throughout the whole world."

## 84 | CHRIST WILL RETURN

The angelic promise that Christ will return is not only the capstone of the Exercises. It is the goal of Christianity. If there is one outstanding feature of the Christian religion, it is its clear finality or purposefulness.

Everything in our lives is part of the mysterious providence of God.

Already in the Principle and Foundation, St. Ignatius reminded us that there is no such thing as chance in our lives. Everything has a divinely ordained purpose, leading us day by day and moment by moment to our final purpose, which is to reach Jesus Christ when he returns to call us to himself.

**His coming at our bodily death.** Christ foretold that he would come as a thief in the night.

The language is symbolic, but it is not cryptic. As the Church has always understood this, Our Lord is the one who will call us out of time into eternity at what we commonly call death. But it is not we who die. It is our bodies that will die, and decay, and be delayed in their reunion with our souls. To coin a phrase, this is Christ's first Second Coming. His first return to each one of us individually.

**His coming on the last day.** However, he will come once again at the general judgment on the last day of the earthly human family. The most detailed account of this is given by St. Matthew, where Christ foretells his coming to judge the human race.

Why this general judgment? So that the mercy and justice of God might be publicly manifest, but also that the consequences of human actions might be universally recognized.

Every moral action we perform has consequences on and on

until the end of time. At the last judgment, therefore, these consequences will be revealed—not to humiliate the repentant but to justify the divine justice and to glorify the mercy of God.

**Spiritual implications.** The one basic implication stressed by Christ is to be ready. This says more than being prepared for death, which can come at any moment when we least expect it. To be ready for Christ's coming is not only a warning. It is a reminder to be always on the alert for the constant visitations of his grace. Every actual grace we receive as a holy thought or holy desire is a coming of Christ into our lives. We are to be very watchful for these visitations and respond to them with generous cooperation on our part. If we are, and in the measure that we respond, we shall be prepared for the Lord's coming to call us to our final destiny.

## Maxim of St. Justin Martyr

"The prophets have foretold two comings of Christ: the one which has already taken place was that of a dishonored and suffering man; the other coming will take place, as it is predicted, when he shall gloriously come from heaven with his angelic army, when he shall also raise to life the bodies of all the men that ever were, shall cloak the worthy with immortality, and shall relegate the wicked, subject to sensible pain for all eternity, into the eternal fire with the evil demons."

# 29

# Contemplation for Divine Love

THROUGHOUT THE SPIRITUAL EXERCISES there is one pervading truth of faith, the love of God for the human race.

It is not surprising, then, that St. Ignatius would have us concentrate in a special contemplation on divine love. He calls it a contemplation because its purpose is not so much intellectual conviction as volitional affection. He assumes that we do love God. But our love should become stronger. In theological terms, we are to grow in the supernatural virtue of charity.

In one sense this is the focus of every meditation of the Exercises. Here we are providing a practical method of living out the Exercises until the dawn of eternity. Whatever else we do in life, whatever decisions we have made, or resolutions we have reached, the heart of the spiritual life is our responsive love for God in return for his great love for us.

As Ignatius sees this, it means that as we become habitually aware of God's goodness to us, we develop the corresponding habit of loving God in everything we do.

Our plan for the three meditations on divine love is to make one meditation each on St. Ignatius' understanding of love, his analysis of the ways in which God has been loving us, and his classic prayer, "Take, O Lord, and receive."

## 85 THE MANIFESTATION AND ESSENCE OF LOVE

There is surely no word in any language with more divergent meanings than "love." The reason for this is the simple fact that we love what we think is good. But the meaning of "good" depends on our philosophy of life. And beyond each one's philosophy is the mind and will of God who always knows what is truly good and always wants us to conform to his mind and choose according to his will.

St. Ignatius' contemplation on love was eminently practical. Before the close of the Exercises, he wanted to give us some guidelines on how to attain even the highest reaches of love for God. That is why he began the contemplation with an explanation of the meaning of love.

**Showing one's love in deeds.** There is divine pragmatism in Christ's teaching that is reflected in every paragraph of the Spiritual Exercises. Time and again Jesus insisted that love is indeed interior in its source. But if it is genuine, it shows itself in action. The parable of the Prodigal Son is only one of a score of revelations on this subject in the Gospels.

**Love consists in mutual sharing.** As St. Ignatius explains it, "The lover gives and shares with the beloved what he possesses or something of that which he has or is able to give." This mutual sharing is not only, or mainly, of something material. It is especially in sharing spiritual possessions like knowledge or channels of grace.

**Mutual "sharing" with God.** Even as we say this, we must immediately qualify the idea of sharing between ourselves and God.

Although the language is familiar, yet absolutely speaking whatever God gives us, he does not actually share. He does not part with anything or lose anything in giving us whatever we possess.

On our part, too, whatever we give to God does not enrich

him in any way. He is infinite in his perfections and cannot gain anything from anyone no matter how generous a person is towards God.

It is here that the mystery of the Incarnation takes on such profound significance. Since God has become human, we can literally give him what, except for our generosity, he would not have received, namely our love.

## Maxims of the Saints

"Thou hast made us for thyself, and the heart of man is restless until it finds its rest in thee." St. Augustine

"Late have I loved thee, O Beauty so ancient and so new; late have I loved thee! For behold thou wert within me, and I outside and in my unliveliness fell upon those lovely things that thou hast made. Thou wert within me and I was not with thee."
St. Augustine

"Love is sufficient by itself, it pleases by itself and for its own sake. It is like a merit and itself its own recompense. Love seeks neither cause nor fruit beyond itself. Its fruit is its use. I love because I love; I love that I may love. Love, then, is a reality. It is the only one of all the movements, feelings, and affections of the soul in which the creature is able to respond to its Creator, though not upon equal terms, and to repay like with like." St. Bernard

<table>
<tr><td>86</td><td>GRATITUDE AS THE FOUNDATION AND MODEL OF OUR LOVE OF GOD</td></tr>
</table>

The relationship of gratitude and love is closer than most people realize. This is deeper than the psychological connection between receiving a favor from someone and wanting to reciprocate the favor received.

Here it is God whom we are to love. We know we cannot give God anything that he does not already possess. This can blind us to the fact although he does not need anything, yet he wants what we alone can give him, namely our love.

In order to be inspired to love God, we must become aware of his goodness, not in the abstract but specifically to us.

**The blessings and favors from God.** It is impossible to estimate all the gifts that the human race has received from the divine bounty. Except for God who freely chose to create humanity, there would not be a human race. Except for God becoming human, there would have been no redemption.

I must make this realization of God's goodness personal to me. "I will ponder with great affection how much God Our Lord has done for me and how much he has given me what he possesses."

Nor is that all. God has not only been giving me creatures, including myself, as the creation of his love. "The same Lord desires to give himself to me," a gift which on earth is the possession of his grace and in heaven the Beatific Vision.

This should evoke from me the question of "what I ought to offer the divine majesty, that is, all I possess and myself with it."

**God dwells in his creatures.** We know from reason and on faith that God is in everything which he gives us. The same almighty love that brought us and the rest of creation into existence continues dwelling within creation. Otherwise, everything would lapse into the nothingness from which it was originally made.

Nor is this a mere passive exercise of divine power enabling creatures to continue in existence. It is God whose loving omnipotence continually enables his creatures to live and act and exercise their powers.

Then I ask myself. How wholeheartedly do I put myself into what I am doing for God? How much of myself do I expend in carrying out the divine will in my life?

**God works and labors for me.** As far as human language allows us to say it, "God works and labors for me in all creatures upon the face of the earth."

This is no figure of speech. God is exercising the same infinite power to sustain me in being and activity as he exercised when he first created me. He is doing so with the same selfless love and with the same total liberty.

"Then I reflect on myself," and ask myself: How much effort do I put into what I am doing for God? Do I really exert myself? Do I labor at what I am doing for him?

God became man out of love for me. He became tired, even exhausted. He suffered and died in his tireless love for me. How generous am I in my exhausting labor out of love for him? How ready am I to suffer for him, who, having joy set before him, chose the cross out of love for me?

In all of these reflections, I remind myself that these gifts of God's love for me are so many "blessings and gifts." We may use the strange expression that God descends to us in his love. Omnipotence condescends to come down to us. We pray that the Holy Spirit may pour down his blessings on us.

In every case we are trying to express the inexpressible: that God, the only necessary being, loves us, his creatures who, except for his love, would not even exist.

**Maxims of the Saints**

"We are led to give thanks to God because seeing that God is the Creator of all things, it is certain that all that we are and all that we have come from God."   St. Thomas Aquinas

"That we must recognize and acknowledge every good as a gift and that even the patient endurance of suffering for Christ's sake is of God. That we should not accept in silence the blessings of God but return thanks for them."   St. Basil

## 87 | THE *SUSCIPE*

All the historical evidence indicates that St. Ignatius was the original author of the *Suscipe*. It is the last formal prayer of the

Spiritual Exercises. It not only capsulizes all the preceding meditations. It synthesizes them in a single prayerful oblation to God and is meant to be memorized and recited daily by everyone who has made an Ignatian retreat.

There is more than academic value in giving the original Latin text of this prayer. One reason is that no translation can ever do full justice to exactly what the words of the *Suscipe* say.

> *Suscipe, Domine, universam meam libertatem. Accipe memoriam, intellectum, atque voluntatem omnem. Quidquid habeo vel possideo mihi largitus es; id tibi totum restituo, ac tuae prorsus voluntati trado gubernandum. Amorem tui solum cum gratia tua mihi dones, et dives sum satis, hec aliud quidquam ultra posco.*

Our meditation on the *Suscipe* will be on its three main parts, each of which has its own distinctive theme.

**Giving God everything.** The first two sentences of the *Suscipe* are a total offering of oneself to God: "Receive, O Lord, all my liberty. Take my memory, my understanding, and my entire will."

There is a difference between "Receive" and "Take" in the two offerings. "Receive" here means giving to God our entire liberty. Whereas "take" rather means surrendering everything over which we have voluntary control. These are mainly the three faculties of our soul: the memory, the understanding, and the will.

Why the distinction between offering God our freedom and telling him to take our memory, understanding, and our entire will? The reason is that if we are truly sincere in sacrificing our freedom to God, we are implicitly giving him dominion over the three highest possessions we have:

- our memory of the past;
- our understanding of the present;
- our will with its desires and hopes and loves for the future.

We see, therefore, that the heart of the spiritual life and almost a definition of sanctity is to offer up, in sacrifice of our own preferences, our entire free will.

**Returning to God what he has given to me.** We are dealing here with an unfathomable mystery. It is the mystery of human freedom. We are actually able to return to God everything that he has given to us.

What are we telling God? We are saying, "Whatsoever I have or hold, you have given to me; I give it all back to you and surrender it wholly to be governed by your will."

This may sound strange, but the truth it expresses is profound. Unlike the irrational creation, we are able to:

- Know with our minds what we possess.
- Recognize that all our possessions are so many constant gifts from God.
- Decide on how we are going to use these divine gifts.
- Choose to use them according to the will of God.

Of course, we are physically able to choose to do our own will contrary to the divine will. But we are morally free to do only the will of God, no matter what self-sacrifice this may require.

**Ask only for God's love and his grace.** What do I ask from God in return? "Give me only your love and your grace, and I am rich enough and ask for nothing more."

This is the climax of the *Suscipe*. We know what Scripture quotes God as saying, "I love those who love me..." (Prv 8:17a, JB). God is never outdone in generosity. We move one step towards him, and he moves a thousand miles towards us.

What bears emphasis, however, is that we must leave it entirely up to God how he will reward our generosity to him. In the language of St. Ignatius, all we ask for is that he give us his love and his grace. This bestowal of his love and his grace is certain, depending on our self-sacrifice to him. But the form that God's love and grace will take is up to him to decide. We are not bargaining with God as though we expect from him a salary of consolations for doing his will. No, we are satisfied to believe, on faith, that our sacrifice of self to him will be infallibly rewarded by his loving grace to us.

## Maxims of the Saints

"Not only in works but also in faith, God has given man freedom of the will." St. Ireneus

"We have freedom to do good or evil; yet to make choice of evil is not to use but to abuse our freedom." St. Francis de Sales

# 30

## Three Methods of Prayer

THERE IS GOOD REASON WHY ST. IGNATIUS gave the Three Methods of Prayer as a kind of addendum to the Spiritual Exercises. Whatever else the Exercises are, they are a coordinated, logically structured period of concentrated prayer.

Thus the three methods are in the nature of an overview of the Exercises with the purpose of putting them into daily use for the rest of one's life.

Why spend the final day on these methods of prayer? In order to plan one's spiritual life on its most important aspect, namely, how to live in the presence of God and communicate with him as often and for as long as circumstances will provide.

These methods are very definite, specific, and practical. They are intended as guidelines for the practice of mental prayer. They correspond to Christ's answer to his disciples when they asked him, "... Lord, teach us to pray..." (Lk 11:1b).

| 88 | ON THE DECALOGUE, SEVEN CAPITAL SINS, POWERS OF THE SOUL, AND THE SENSES |
|----|---|

As explained by St. Ignatius, this is not so much a method of prayer as a way of disposing oneself for acceptance by God.

The focus of reflection is to see where I have failed and how I can be more faithful in observing the commandments of God, avoiding the capital sins and using my mental and sense faculties in the service of God.

**The Ten Commandments.** Surprisingly, Ignatius does not stress what may be called an examination of conscience. He assumes that being human we have sinned against some or all of the Ten Commandments. He tells us to "beg for a perfect understanding of them in order to observe them better and glorify and praise the divine majesty more."

To get some taste of what this means, it is advised taking the first commandment and spending some time reflecting on:

- What does the first commandment oblige when it declares, "I, the Lord, am your God.... You shall not have other gods besides me"? (Ex 20:1a, 3)
- How well have I observed this basic law of our existence which commands us to recognize only the one true God as Lord and Master of the universe?
- How can I improve my practice of the first commandment by more clearly seeing God in every experience of my life and more faithfully conforming my will to his?

**Capital sins.** Do the same with the capital sins. They are pride, lust, anger, covetousness, envy, sloth, and gluttony. Any one or several of these sins can be the subject of my prayer. Thus, I may take pride as my sample meditation.

- What do I understand by pride as inordinate self-esteem?
- How have I failed in humility, especially in humility of mind?
- How, practically speaking, can I become more humble?

It is a matter of experience that the sins to which I am most naturally prone and most frequently commit are God's way of telling me what virtues I most need.

In this connection the one making the Exercises should seriously plan on making a daily examen of conscience. Become familiar with St. Ignatius' explanation of the general and particular examens as given in the first week of the Spiritual Exercises.

**Powers of the soul and senses of the body.** For St. Ignatius the three basic powers of the soul are the memory, understanding, and the will.

As before, I ask myself how am I using my memory—what kind of past experiences do I keep in mind or allow myself to dwell on? Custody of the memory is elementary to growth in holiness.

The same with my understanding. What control do I have of my thoughts? Do I seriously discipline my intellect? Writing one's thoughts in a daily journal is highly recommended.

So, too, the will. How much do I really use my will and try to make acts of the will in prayerful union with the will of God?

The same process should be followed in meditating on the use of my bodily senses: the eyes, ears, mouth, nostrils, and touch. All are divine gifts to be used according to God's will.

We do not often think, though we should, of worshiping God with our bodies. They are temples of the Holy Spirit. They are under the power of our free will. They are wonderful means of glorifying God. But we must make ourselves aware of these facts in order to serve Our Lord in soul *and* body even as he glorified the Father with his bodily senses and powers.

## Maxim of St. Augustine

"To teach these grades [of the soul] to anyone, let the acts of the soul from the lowest to the highest be called, first, animation; second, sensation; third, art; fourth, virtue; fifth, tranquility; sixth, approach; seventh, contemplation.

"They can be named also in this way: of the body; through the body; about the body; towards itself; towards God; in God.

"Or again in this way: beautifully of another; beautifully through another; beautifully about another; beautifully towards a beautiful; beautifully in a beautiful; beautifully towards Beauty; beautifully in Beauty."

| 89 | CONTEMPLATING THE MEANING OF EACH WORD OF A PRAYER |

St. Ignatius makes a wise observation in introducing this method, "One may kneel, or sit," he says, "as may be better suited to his disposition and more conducive to devotion." The important thing is for the mind to be alert.

Any standard vocal prayer may be used. It can be the Our Father, or the Hail Mary, or the Apostles' Creed, according to a person's choice. Some practical recommendations include:

- First vocally pronounce the word or phrase of the prayer.
- Then meditate on its meaning as long as the mind is being enlightened and the will inspired.
- Spend as much time on the word or term as desired, up to an hour, and finish the rest of the prayer in the usual way.

Our choice here is the first part of the Hail Mary. It is the Angelic Salutation of the Archangel Gabriel to the Blessed Virgin at Nazareth.

**Hail Mary.** This was no casual greeting of Our Lady by the angel of the annunciation. It was nothing less than a revealed imperative. The heavenly messenger told her, "Rejoice," much as the angels of Bethlehem told the shepherds they were receiving the good news (or gospel) of great joy.

The name "Mary" is the equivalent of the English "Lady," or in Latin *Domina*. A perfect synonym would be "Queen." And such she was to become since the child she would conceive and bear was to be the King of kings and the Lord of lords.

**Full of grace.** No other words than these express what the Archangel Gabriel addressed to Our Lady. This is the judgment of St. Jerome, whom Pope St. Damasus commissioned to translate the Bible into the Latin Vulgate. Ever since, the Church has spoken of Mary as *gratia plena*, which literally means "full of grace." As St. Jerome explained, "Indeed full of grace, for to others it is given in portions, but on Mary its fullness is showered." If we ask how Mary is "full of grace," we say because:

- She was conceived in the friendship of God without original sin.
- She remained sinless all through her life.
- She conceived and gave birth to the Son of God.
- She was declared by her Son to be the Mother of the Church, which is the universal sacrament or channel of grace to the whole human race.

**The Lord is with thee.** This is a direct quotation from the angel at Nazareth. Of no one can it be said that the Lord was or is with them as was true of Mary.

- The Lord of the universe was within her during the nine months of her being with child.
- The Lord was with her in the most intimate sense possible as she nursed and cared for him as a child.
- The Lord was with her during the thirty years at Nazareth.
- The Lord was with her in spirit during his ministry in Palestine.
- The Lord was with her physically as she stood under the cross on Calvary.
- The Lord is now with her in her glorified body, channelling his grace through her intercession to all the children of the human family.

## Maxims of St. Augustine

"We should not imagine, as some do, that prolonged prayer is the same thing as much speaking; many words are one thing; long continued experience of devotion quite another."

"When you pray to God with psalms and hymns, meditate in your heart on what you are saying with your voice."

# 90 | MEASURED RHYTHMIC RECITATION

To some people the third method of prayer must seem unusual.

This is what St. Ignatius recommends. "With each breath or respiration," he teaches, "one should pray mentally while saying a simple word of the Our Father or other prayer that is being recited in such a way that from one breath to another a single word is said."

This recommendation should not be taken lightly. It associates the spontaneous bodily rhythm of breathing with the spiritual rhythm of praying. Three aspects of this practice deserve to be singled out for reflection.

**The essence of mental prayer.** St. Ignatius is mainly concerned with the activity of the mind during what is appropriately called mental prayer.

While associating each word of a vocal prayer with each breath, we are told that "the attention is chiefly directed to the meaning of the word, to the person who is addressed, to our own lowliness, or the difference between the greatness of the person and our own littleness."

This statement is priceless. We are being told by one of the Church's greatest mystics what is the essence of mental prayer. It is simply paying attention to any aspect of our conscious communication with God.

**Value of understanding our prayer.** It cannot be too often said that our prayer should be intelligible. In other words, we should know what we are saying when we are praying.

Rhythmic recitation is part of the worship of many world religions. What is crucial, however, is that rhythmic prayer should be intelligible. It is not as Christ described the pagan practice of just reciting words.

**Prayer is the breath of the believing soul.** More than one saint has described prayer as the respiration of the soul.

We take for granted that the body must breathe in order to stay alive. So, too, the soul must breathe to stay supernaturally alive. Therefore, what breathing is to the natural life of the body, praying is to the supernatural life of the soul. We cannot remain physically alive without constant rhythmic breathing in air. Neither, on a higher level, can we remain spiritually alive without constant, even rhythmic, breathing in of divine grace by the practice of regular prayer.

## Maxims of the Saints

"In a single day I have prayed as many as a hundred times and in the night almost as often." St. Patrick

"All that should be sought for in the exercise of prayer is conformity of our will with the divine will, in which consists the highest perfection." St. Teresa of Avila

"Prayer is conversation with God." St. Clement of Alexandria

# Another Book of Interest by Servant Publications

## Healing the Original Wound
*Reflections on the Full Meaning of Salvation*

### Benedict Groeschel, C.F.R.

Father Benedict Groeschel invites us to explore the astonishing mystery of God's loving plan for us. He points out that God has showered grace upon grace on the human race. Sometimes it comes in buckets. Sometimes in torrents. Yet often we feel only the thinnest trickle. Many times we suffer through a severe drought. We all hunger to know more about God and our own destiny.

*Healing the Original Wound* is a book about our journey toward God, our journey from the personal hell of sin and alienation toward the paradise of being held in the "Everlasting Arms of God," of being restored to the divine image implanted on our souls. It is a book for anyone who knows something about the imperative need, the restlessness, the hunger we all have, to find unfailing love in the brief reality that we call our lives.                                             **$8.99**